D0946352

Disrupting the Status Quo

Status Quo

Northwell Health's Mission to
Reshape the Future of Health Care

Endorsements

Advance praise for Disrupting the Status Quo: Northwell Health's Mission to Reshape the Future of Health Care

"The story of Michael J. Dowling and Northwell Health should be read by anyone who hopes to understand the challenges faced by hospitals in this turbulent era. It shows how one great hospital system and [is] managing change, and helping to lead the transformation of American healthcare."

Toby Cosgrove, MD
CEO and President, Cleveland Clinic

"The book is brilliant! It will help you see into the future and serve as a leadership text for years to come."

Maureen Bisognano
President Emerita and Senior Fellow Institute for Healthcare Improvement

"This is a book about change. Northwell Health's reshaping of itself as a high quality consumer focused population health based institution is an Operational Roadmap for the future of America's healthcare delivery system. The Northwell story is the beginning of tomorrow."

Stephen Berger
Chairman Commission on Health Care Facilities in the 21st Century

"By combining a caring mission with a commitment to learning and innovation, Northwell Health and CEO Michael Dowling are leading the future of healthcare."

Jeff Immelt
Chairman and CEO, GE

Disrupting the Status Quo

Northwell Health's Mission to Reshape the Future of Health Care

By

Charles Kenney

CRC Press
Taylor & Francis Group
Boca Raton London New York

CRC Press is an imprint of the
Taylor & Francis Group, an **informa** business

CRC Press
Taylor & Francis Group
6000 Broken Sound Parkway NW, Suite 300
Boca Raton, FL 33487-2742

© 2017 by Charles Kenney
CRC Press is an imprint of Taylor & Francis Group, an Informa business

No claim to original U.S. Government works

Printed on acid-free paper

International Standard Book Number-13: 978-1-138-06841-4 (Hardback)

Library of Congress Cataloging-in-Publication Data

Names: Kenney, Charles, author.
Title: Disrupting the status quo : Northwell Health's mission to reshape the future of health care / Charles Kenney.
Description: Boca Raton : Taylor & Francis, 2017. | "A CRC title, part of the Taylor & Francis imprint, a member of the Taylor & Francis Group, the academic division of T&F Informa plc." | Includes index.
Identifiers: LCCN 2017005036 | ISBN 9781138068414 (hardback : alk. paper)
Subjects: LCSH: Health promotion. | Integrated delivery of health care.
Classification: LCC RA427.8 .K47 2017 | DDC 362.1--dc23
LC record available at https://lccn.loc.gov/2017005036

Visit the Taylor & Francis Web site at
http://www.taylorandfrancis.com

and the CRC Press Web site at
http://www.crcpress.com

Printed and bound in the United States of America by Sheridan

Contents

Author vii

Preface: A Humbling Journey ix

1 Mission...1
   Limerick 4

2 Growing Pains: Building an Integrated Network ...15
   Culture Clash..20
   Mosaic...24
   Level Playing Field 27

3 Learning Obsession 29
   Learning from Top Gun..37
   The Power of Simulation 39

4 Redefining Medical Education: Creating the
   Hofstra Northwell School of Medicine..................59
   From Abraham Flexner to Michael Dowling....................59
   Audacious Ambition..65
   Learning from Other Medical Schools 68
   One-on-One with Physician Mentors..............................76
   Assess Knowledge-in-Action, Not Memorization..............82
   Case-Based Curriculum..86

5 Emergency Preparedness......................................95
   Mission.. 111

6 What Does Quality Care Look Like?......................**115**
Caring for Vincent...116
Training as a Team, Working as a Team.......................122
Burnout...135

7 Rory **141**
Four Life-Saving Steps......................................150
Sepsis Mortality Cut in Half................................161
Rory's Legacy...164
A Mother's Plea...166

8 Care Value...**171**
A New Company...177

9 Beyond the Horizon.................................**189**
The Road Ahead..189
Cold Spring Harbor Laboratories............................ 200
Bioelectronic Medicine 204

Index..**219**

Author

Charles Kenney is Chief Journalist at Northwell Health and Executive Editor of the *Northwell Health Series on Health Care Innovation.* He worked as an editor and reporter for 15 years at *The Boston Globe* and served as host of a weekly political interview program on the CBS television affiliate in Boston. He is the author of many books including *The Best Practice: How the New Quality Movement Is Transforming Medicine* (2008), which the *New York Times* described as "the first large-scale history of the quality movement." He is the author of *Transforming Health Care: Virginia Mason Medical Center's Pursuit of the Perfect Patient Experience (2010),* for which he was awarded the 2012 Shingo Research and Professional Publication Award. He serves on the faculty of the Institute for Healthcare Improvement in Cambridge, Massachusetts.

Preface

A Humbling Journey

"In healthcare you see difficult things and beautiful things other people do not see and you learn things others do not know."

Michael Dowling

The world has changed in immeasurable ways over the past 2000 years, yet the core belief among people to care for the sick has remained a defining human value. Jesus sent his disciples out to both preach the gospel and heal the sick and through the millennia, people of all faith traditions have sought to do the same. Throughout human history, health care has been a selfless, noble calling. With advances in science and technology, medicine is more effective than ever. At the same time, with the stakes in human life so high, it is among the most humbling professions. It is humbling to deal with people at the most extreme moments of their lives, to be with them in their sorrow—and in their joy, as well—both overpowering in their different ways. It is humbling, in part, because success is often so elusive. While triumph is a daily reality in nearly every hospital worldwide, so, too, is failure.

As a caregiver, for example, you believe that you provide some of the finest inpatient care anywhere only to discover that the leading killer of hospital patients worldwide is twice as prevalent in your own hospitals as it should be. You believe that your programs designed to teach doctors, nurses and others about new ways of delivering care are up to date until you find that people in other industries are light years ahead. You know that central to your mission is to care for the neediest people among us and you believe that you have done well in this area, and then one day your attention is drawn to a neighborhood in your home city where hundreds of thousands of people have minimal, if any, access to a clinic, doctor, or even to a pharmacy.

It is humbling—and more than a little embarrassing, in fact—to realize that the health care industry of which you are a part is consuming nearly one in every five dollars of goods and services produced by the nation each year and, as a consequence, depriving worthy programs in education, infrastructure, national defense, and the environment from needed funding. Surely it is humbling when you realize that just in the past few years the essential mission of the job has changed. For 2000 years the mission was healing, but now it is better defined as the pursuit of health—and the difference, as you will see in this book—is enormous. While once the mission was to wait inside a clinic or hospital for sick people to arrive and to cure them, the mission now is to go out into the community and head off disease, to manage and control it. What used to be the ideal scenario for a health system—having lots of sick patients in the hospital—has been turned on its head. Now the ideal is to have lots of healthy people in their homes.

We are in the midst of perhaps the most turbulent period in the history of modern medicine. At such a moment it is wise to gauge the broader context of change. Isaiah Berlin, the brilliant Oxford philosopher who died in 1997 at age 88, would have understood health care today. Among Berlin's many contributions to modern thought was his seminal essay "The Hedgehog and the Fox."[1] In his attempt to analyze some of history's great minds, Berlin was inspired by an ancient Greek poet who observed that "the fox knows many things, but the hedgehog knows one big thing." In Berlin's essay, which has found a worldwide audience in the many millions since it was published six decades ago, he applied this definition to great thinkers through the ages.

Berlin's analysis is useful in helping us understand the evolution of health care in the modern world. Not so many years ago the industry was all about being a hedgehog who knew one thing—healing—extremely well. Rapidly, however, in recent years, it has become clear that health care is an industry best suited to the fox, for health care today means knowing many more things than medicine. It means knowing the intricacies of technology, finance, risk, public health, and population health management. It means figuring out how to build a system that achieves scale and leverage in the marketplace; it means providing emergency services even under the most adverse circumstances; it means identifying additional revenue streams to offset reductions from Medicare and Medicaid; it means learning, through painful trial and error, how to provide care to the neediest in society even as government payments decline. It means learning how to push outside the clinic to improve the overall health of individuals and communities by working on determinants of health beyond the typical medical practice.

The only way to keep up is to learn continually; to learn new and better ways of doing everything and that is what this book is all about. Continuous learning defines the fox and leads to breakthroughs and innovations that matter. The process itself is humbling. When you commit to learn you begin by conceding your own lack of knowledge and this can be difficult for highly educated people like the doctors, nurses, and others who populate the health care world. There are painful stumbles along the way and the realization that learning while doing can be somewhat overwhelming. It actually is somewhat like drinking from a fire hose.

All of us with a stake in the industry that is health care—and that includes everyone in our country—can clearly see the status quo is blowing sky high right before our eyes and with that explosion comes change, uncertainty, and much anxiety. Patients and families worry, *will I be able to get care for myself, for my kids? Will I be able to afford it?* Doctors, nurses and other caregivers wonder, *when is all this change too much change? When are we being asked to do more than is humanly possible to do?* Those who pay for care—governments at all levels, employers, individuals—wonder *will the rising cost spiral ever end?* Harvard's Michael Porter has written widely on health care arguing that it is time "for a fundamentally new strategy," but what, exactly? Where is the industry headed? What do the changes and the turbulence mean for patients, doctors, nurses? The good news is that we, as an industry, are figuring out ways to get better at delivering quality care. Measurement is key. "For hundreds of years in medicine there was no data," says Dr. Lawrence Smith, the Physician-in-Chief at Northwell Health. "You couldn't compare the performance of one physician to another or one hospital to another but now we have moved rapidly into this data-driven world so that we can measure ourselves."

Disrupting the Status Quo is the product of a learning journey—a humbling, sometimes disappointing, often exhilarating, and always revealing learning journey—through one of the most turbulent periods in medical history. This book inaugurates the *Northwell Health Series on Health Care Innovation*. This first book, along with subsequent titles in the series, aims to provide a deeper, clearer understanding of what is happening in health care and why; to help illuminate a pathway forward for patients and caregivers most of all, but also for policy-makers and the employers and others who pay for care. "Being in healthcare provides you with a perspective unlike any other industry," says Michael Dowling, Northwell CEO. "You see difficult things and beautiful things other people do not see and you learn things others do not know." The idea of this book is to share with you what we at Northwell have seen and learned with the hope that it helps continue the age-old tradition of doing all we can to comfort and heal all people.

Endnote

1. "The Hedgehog and the Fox: An essay on Tolstoy's view of history"; published by Weidenfeld & Nicolson, United Kingdom, 1953.

Chapter 1

Mission

"Saint Francis, Buddha, Muhammad, Maimonides all spoke the truth when they said the only way to serve yourself is to serve others."

Mario Cuomo

"Our real mission."

On a sparkling June day in 2016, a couple of hundred leaders from Northwell Health—doctors, nurses, researchers, administrators of all stripes—convened in Montauk, New York, for several days of reflection and discussion. In itself, the gathering was not unusual. What was, unusual, however, was the agenda—for the conversations and presentations were *not* about Northwell; not about its 21 hospitals, 550 ambulatory centers, $11 billion budget, or its 61,000 employees. Instead, the discussions and presentations were about five hospitals that are not part of the Northwell organization in communities where Northwell has no presence.

The Montauk gathering focused on the poorest areas of Brooklyn and, in particular, on five hospitals in financial difficulty. Michael Dowling, Northwell's Chief Executive Officer, drew his colleagues' attention to these Brooklyn neighborhoods that are home to a half million people, most black or Hispanic. More than 90 percent of these residents have no commercial insurance, Dowling said, and rely upon Medicaid. This is an area where it is difficult to find a drug store and next to impossible to find an ambulatory clinic. The problem, Dowling said, was that these hospitals were in danger of going under. In search of a solution, New York state leaders turned to Northwell. "We have an obligation to help," Dowling told the gathering. "To do things others walk away from. We cannot walk away. We cannot say it is not our problem." These Brooklyn neighborhoods were facing "a complex calamity of social issues," Dr. Lawrence Smith, Northwell's Physician-in-Chief, told the Montauk gathering. None of the other major health systems in the state, he added, "want to touch this but somebody has to and it will be us." The Northwell team took on the challenge to develop a plan to stabilize these Brooklyn hospitals to improve quality, access, financial stability and the health of the population. Part of the challenge was that most people outside these neighborhoods "stay on the highway and never see it," Dr. Smith continued. "We all need to get off the highway and figure out what's going on all around us so we understand what our real mission is."

Real mission? Wasn't that to treat patients? To heal the sick? For the people gathered in Montauk that was only part of the story. The real mission, as defined by Dowling, Smith and their colleagues went beyond a determination to heal the sick. The real mission aspires to equity, a concept as elusive in twenty-first century America as political harmony. It aspires to the concept enunciated by Dr. Paul Farmer, the founder of Partners in Health, that "the idea that some lives matter less is the root of all that is wrong with the world ..." It was through equity that health was achievable in all of society but surely in these Brooklyn neighborhoods where equity was as scarce as a pharmacy. "We need to make sure that every person who touches our care system has the complete care they need, delivered with equity and quality no matter where they come from or their ability to pay," says Smith. "That means great care for poor and middle class families, for wealthy people, but everybody can't be treated the same to get the same outcomes. The best care comes from understanding the social context of illness. If you want to be the caregiver of a region, part of the mission is to do whatever you need to do to make sure that your presence improves the health of the region. *Everybody's* health. There are hidden health issues everywhere, different social determinants of health and you bear responsibility to work on those. As the standard bearer of health care in a region you have an obligation to look not just at the people who come in the door with active medical problems, but to look at all the reasons why the health of the people in your area deteriorates."

The *real mission* recognizes that good health is the result of a complex set of determinants that exist far outside the clinic walls, determinants that include poverty, employment, food, education, and housing. When you listen to Dowling, Smith, Chief Operating Officer Mark Solazzo and their colleagues, you realize that the real mission for Northwell is to improve the health—in its broadest definition—of all people in the community while making care more affordable.

From a certain perspective, Northwell looks very much like other large health care organizations: It includes hospitals, clinics, physicians, and a research institute. Viewed from another perspective, however, the system is an outlier. Dowling and his leadership team started a medical school and a nursing school from scratch, created the first (and one of the only) corporate universities in health care, built one of the largest private emergency response systems in the United States, and started a new health plan. "We are in the hospital and ambulatory care business," says Dowling, "but we are also in the education business, the insurance business, the research business, but above everything, we are in the health business. Our responsibility is the health of everybody who lives in our communities."

In Montauk, listening to the presentations and late-night conversations, you might think you were at a social services conference, maybe a collaboration among government, community agencies, and perhaps even a church group. And you might well wonder, *how did this happen*? How did an organization that started with the merger of Long Island hospitals become this vast hybrid of science, medicine, and mission? How did these seemingly disparate elements coalesce to create this large, powerful, even unique health care system? The answers can only be found if you look back—back before Dowling joined Northwell and was working for his mentor, Governor Mario M. Cuomo; back even before that, when Michael Dowling was growing up in Ireland.

Limerick

As a boy in Limerick in the 1950s and '60s, when Michael Dowling wanted to get his mother's attention, he would tap his foot on the dirt floor of the family cottage and, somehow, his mother would feel the vibration. Michael's mother was deaf, likely the result of a medical error when she was just six years old. His father, arthritic and swollen with pain, was unable to work beyond his early 40s. Home for the seven-member Dowling family was a three-room, thatched roof structure with no running water, plumbing, or electricity, where Michael's mother scrubbed laundry on a washboard, sewed worn garments for her children, and cooked in a huge iron pot in a central fireplace.

Michael was the eldest of five children, born at home in 1949. From an early age he was a sponge, absorbing everything around him, observing as keenly as his mother did, with the added ability to listen. He possessed a ferocious capacity for work which was evident by the time he was ten years old and toiling in the fields and sheds of local farms. He was a ruggedly physical boy, but cerebral, as well, with a natural curiosity and a desire to learn—from other people, of course, but also, early on, from borrowed books read by candlelight. His desire for education—more like a compulsion—required what was in shortest supply in the Dowling household—money. Thus, did his pursuit of work become an animating force in Dowling's life. During summers in high school he made his way from Limerick to Crawley, England, south of London, traveling by bus, ferry, then bus again, working as a laborer and saving virtually everything he earned for courses at University College in Cork, 60 miles from Limerick. He hitched a ride to Cork on a milk truck believing that his destiny was to become a teacher—a belief born of the reality that the only college-educated people he encountered growing up were teachers. As apocryphal as it sounds, the truth is that when he registered freshman year at Cork he found himself in a line for "liberal arts" and panicked because he did not know how to draw. For the next four years his time was balanced between academic work and physical labor as a means of paying for college. In pursuit of better paying jobs he followed the well-worn path from Ireland to the shores of America where he found work on the Manhattan docks within sight of the Statue of Liberty. He was eighteen years old and though he did not quite know it yet, he had found his future home. The summer days in Manhattan in the mid-1960s were long and hot and he worked seven days a week, rarely partied, never spent a dollar he could save. Those days, he would later say, were "the happiest moments of my life" because he was able to send money—money that made a difference in the quality of life for his parents and siblings—back to Limerick. The separation from his family was the toughest part. When Dowling was working in the U.S. his contact with his family came about when his parents and siblings would travel from the countryside into the center of the village where there was a telephone booth near the church. "I would write a letter home to tell them that three weeks from the following Saturday at 7:00 o'clock I will call that phone by the church. It took about two weeks for my letter to reach them. And on the appointed day I would call and my family would be standing there. My sister and my brother would always answer the phone. It was really expensive so the calls were brief. Sometimes the phone didn't work back then and I wouldn't get through, but a lot of the time I did and I would talk with my brother and sister and I would hear my mother in the background saying, 'is he okay, is he okay?' She would get on the phone and she would say something, ask how I was but she couldn't hear me. I would say to my sister, 'tell her I'm okay. Tell her everything is fine.' That is how we communicated."

All of this focus on work was, in a fundamental way, joyful for Dowling; joyful because it boosted his sense of confidence along with his determination to do something with his life. It was not as though his entire existence from age ten was consumed with a Dickensian kind of labor. He excelled on the athletic fields where he enjoyed Irish football and a bit of rugby, but his great passion was hurling, the Irish national sport, a frantically-paced game of grueling intensity and no small amount of violence. On the hurling field, Dowling's passion and intensity melded together in an athlete whose natural gifts and seething aggression made him something to behold. Years after he had stopped playing, *The New York Times* reporter Kevin Sack, noting Dowling's aggressive nature, wrote: "That side of Mr. Dowling's temperament may have been honed on the hurling field, where he was a championship player of the rugged Irish pastime that is part field hockey, part soccer. His philosophy on game day, Mr. Dowling said, was that 'if your head gets in the way of my stick, that's your problem'."

"The only way to serve yourself is to serve others."

Soon after graduating from University College Cork in 1970, Dowling headed back to New York for another summer of work on the docks. Often during the summer months, he found himself below decks in a cruise line circumnavigating Manhattan, working in a 100 degree engine room. With his undergraduate degree in hand, he asked around about graduate schools and thus found himself on the doorstep of Fordham University, a Roman Catholic College. Dowling had found an intellectual home, fittingly, within a Jesuit institution. There were few priests left at Fordham when Dowling was there but the smart, driven, no-nonsense Jesuit influence was present nonetheless as Dowling studied public policy, health policy, and welfare policy. Pursuing a master's degree during the day, Dowling worked in the very early mornings cleaning bars in Queens starting at 4 a.m., $50 per week for four bars plus work here and there as a school custodian, a plumber's helper, and back on the west side docks. The money paid for tuition toward his graduate degree in social welfare. Why social welfare? "It was what I knew," he says. He wanted to help people who were struggling, people with crippling arthritis, people who could feel a slight vibration on the floor, but who never heard the music of her children's voices.

While working toward his master's, Dowling caught the eye of department heads and when he graduated they asked him to stay on in an administrative capacity, and then offered him an opportunity to do some teaching as well. He taught classes in public policy, health care policy, and welfare policy, joining the faculty full time in 1975 at the age of twenty-six. He would remain there for the next seven years. While teaching at Fordham, he was well along a PhD track at Columbia, in fact, when an opportunity arose to practice what he taught. Though the doctorate was tantalizingly close, he accepted a position in Albany with the administration of Governor Mario M. Cuomo. Hedging his bets, he checked with leaders at Fordham and was assured that if things did not work out in Albany his faculty position would be waiting for him back on campus.

After a period in which he served as deputy commissioner within the state department of social services, Dowling spent a decade working shoulder-to-shoulder with Mario Cuomo.

With Dowling's office adjacent to the governor's, the two men developed a close working relationship that evolved over time into a friendship sustained through the rest of Cuomo's life. Part of their bond was a shared background. They grew up with a strong work ethic in humble circumstances and both possessed a laser focus on obtaining an education. It so happened that they also played competitive athletics at a high level, Dowling in Ireland, Cuomo in baseball's minor leagues. They were tough men—physically and mentally—and not easily discouraged.

Dowling's job with the state was to oversee an array of programs related to public health and welfare, mental health, substance abuse, alcoholism, aging, social services, insurance, and education. He was one of the leaders with major responsibility for public policy responses to the AIDS epidemic, the homelessness tsunami resulting from deinstitutionalization of state institutions, and the epidemic of crack cocaine. He was never office-bound. He got out and saw what was happening, saw thousands of grandmothers who had worked all their lives now raising grandchildren, elderly women with limited physical capacity with two year olds and four year olds in their care. He saw the parents of these children in treatment programs, on the streets and shelters, and he always returned to his office with the same question: *What can you do about it?* His answer: You protect the safety net; you figure out ways, through times of recession and budget cuts, to do everything possible to help people who needed help. You create a new program providing insurance coverage for children and teenagers in low income families, and you watch the program serve as a model for a national children's health initiative. You revise welfare laws so that while those in need certainly receive assistance, people who are able to work are required to do so—with job training and other foundational support. And then you watch several years later as the much celebrated welfare reform under President Clinton is drawn in some part from your New York plan.

Howard Gold worked directly for Dowling as executive director of the health care advisory board. Gold, who is now Executive Vice President of Northwell, says that while working for Governor Cuomo, Dowling "played a very, very big role in expanding health insurance for children and he was pushing for welfare reform in the 1980s before welfare reform was a thing," says Gold. "Mark Solazzo worked on this with him at the state level also. Michael wanted to turn welfare on its head and create a program[1] that would help a mom with young kids become a productive member of society and find a path out of poverty. He was instrumental in expanding Medicaid across the state, in changing the way that insurance premiums got priced. It was something called community rating and it helped Blue Cross at the expense of some of the big for-profit insurance companies and meant that everybody had to pay the same price which was a fairer way to do it and at the time it was pretty radical—because the big insurance companies really hated that idea." In the *Times* article, Dowling said that "families who are struggling need assistance … [but] it should never undercut the desire of people to help themselves."[2] Governor Cuomo told the *Times* that "nobody knows the poor better than Mike or feels for them more than Mike … Mike knows what poverty is, knows what hard work is." This understanding, according to the *Times* article, was essential to Dowling's efforts "to preserve New York's social safety net when there is increasing political pressure to shrink it … [Dowling] placed his linebacker's frame in the way of the kind of radical cuts in social-service programs being made in states from California to Massachusetts …"

The ethos of the Cuomo Administration was derived from classic social liberalism, embodied in the words of former U.S. Senator and Vice President Hubert Humphrey, who said that the "moral test of government is how that government treats

those who are in the dawn of life, the children; those who are
in the twilight of life, the elderly; and those who are in the
shadows of life, the sick, the needy and the handicapped."

The prevailing political rhetoric of our age strikes a particular theme about government: That it is a dumping ground for
people with limited talent unable to match the entrepreneur-
ial skills that characterize the most dynamic new companies.
While there may be a kernel of truth to this, it is oversimpli-
fied. Yes, government could be reactive, bureaucratic, self-
interested, and worse, but Dowling and his colleagues from
the Cuomo Administration who later joined him at Northwell,
saw a different side of government as well. (Dr. Smith, Mark
Solazzo, and Howard Gold were also, like Dowling, educated
in the Jesuit tradition at Fordham). "A lot of people bashed
government but we understood the good that you could do,"
says Howard Gold. "That's the heart of where Michael is, the
point he starts from. He understands the ethical obligation
and social obligation of running an entity like this. In some
ways, we are taking the place of government, focusing on the
sick and disabled and vulnerable. That is what motivates us.
In some ways, we are stepping into those health and human
services shoes to take care of the health of the community."

Says Dowling: "When you work in government it allows you
to see what others never see—the problems that come to government because none of the other institutions in society can
handle the problem. You see what no other institutions can fix
and you have to understand it and find a way to solve it." As
governor, Cuomo was unyielding in his belief that the foundational element of society was the impulse to serve others. In
a commencement address at Iona College, Cuomo asked the
audience whether "we are the ones to tell [graduates] what their
instructors have tried to teach them for years? That the phi-
losophers were right. That Saint Francis, Buddha, Muhammad,
Maimonides—all spoke the truth when they said the only way
to serve yourself is to serve others; and that Aristotle was right,
before them, when he said the only way to assure yourself

happiness is to learn to give happiness." Cuomo defined his core philosophy saying that "we believe in a single fundamental idea that describes better than most textbooks and any speech that I could write what a proper government should be: the idea of family, mutuality, the sharing of benefits and burdens for the good of all, feeling one another's pain, sharing one another's blessings—reasonably, honestly, fairly, without respect to race, or sex, or geography, or political affiliation."

This was the belief Dowling brought with him from state government to his role, starting in 1995, as chief operating officer of Northwell. This value system was imbued not only in Dowling but also in others who had worked in state government and who went on to play major leadership roles at Northwell, including Howard Gold, Mark Solazzo, Jeff Kraut, executive vice president, and Terry Lynam, senior vice president. Gold characterizes the organization's culture as "consistent with empathetic, public virtues and community values." In some respects, says Gold, governments at various levels pulled back from dealing with certain challenges related to health "and we filled the gap."

"Yes, we will do it."

During a break in the sessions at Montauk, Mark Solazzo, who worked on social services in Albany with Dowling, looked around at his colleagues and talked about the idea, long a motivator in faith-based health care systems, of the "servant leader where the leader is the servant of the mission. There are a lot of times when people don't really live that. Some people and organizations maybe have lost their way sometimes. Here, we are mission-oriented and you get a sense of that from the people. You feel it from them and see it in their actions. There are always exceptions of course, but for the most part people are here for a reason. A number of us came through the government route so for years we have been drawn to health and social services and that mission and sense of values is embodied at Northwell.

Maybe it's contagious maybe because we have been here so long and attract talented people who share that sense of value."

These people were different kinds of leaders of a large health care organization. Look at the leadership team of almost any comparable organization in the U.S. and you will see virtually all physicians and only rarely anyone with a government background. Among the senior leaders at Northwell there is a healthy mix of physician leaders along with men and women trained in other fields who have spent years working in government, which affords a different perspective than prevails at most comparable health care providers.

After 12 years working with Governor Cuomo, who was defeated at the polls in 1994, Dowling joined Empire Blue Cross as senior vice president responsible for the company's relationships with hospitals. He lasted seven months—liked the people, disliked the job: "You sit in an office and look at spreadsheets. You are not where the action is. You are not where the people are." The hierarchical culture—certain furniture for the office of an SVP versus mahogany for the office of an EVP "and all that bullshit"—rubbed him the wrong way. It was at the point, January 1995, that he took the first steps toward forging a new path in health care by accepting a position at North Shore University Hospital on Long Island.

In addition to values, another essential element came to Northwell with Dowling—political savvy; the ability to get things done in a complex environment, and few environments are as contentious and difficult as health care. An ability to build consensus among groups and individuals with conflicting agendas is an essential skill in health care these days. Experience working with many different constituencies in state government, negotiating with unions, government officials at all levels, regulators, legislators, and hospital boards, proves valuable in health care. "I think that is one of the things that is our secret sauce," says Gold. "We have a lot of commonality of experience, we worked together for a long time. We built this place and we are not dispassionate and we may do some things that are not in our financial interest to carry out our strategic mission, and I think that is one of the reasons why we are still successful and highly respected." It was this harder, more pragmatic stuff that Gold talks about that enabled the building of this new entity, a sense of business opportunism, and political savvy—a keener, deeper understanding of the nature of politics and how it applied in the health care universe.

All of this—the size, business perspective, "innovation welded to innate humanism," in Gold's words—is in pursuit of the organization's core mission to bring health to all of the people in all of its communities and this means doing what Dowling and his colleagues are doing in Montauk: Channeling their inner Mario Cuomo and finding ways to help people in need. The complex set of challenges facing the hospitals in the poorer section of Brooklyn was an issue "near and dear to my heart," says Mark Solazzo. "We have the capability to help these residents. They need access to care. They are suffering and it's just wrong and we have the ability to make a difference." Dowling, Solazzo, and Gold "grew up in social services, Medicaid and taking care of individuals who are severely disadvantaged, developmentally disabled," says Jeff Kraut, Northwell executive vice president. "Look at Michael's background, teaching social work at Fordham, working in Albany. Every organization has a social mission but ours is magnified by the experiences and background of our leadership. The state calls Michael and they say, 'we have a problem in Brooklyn. We can't fix it. Insurance companies can't do it. Can you figure out how to do it?' We are uniquely situated; we can take all the players, the providers, the unions, the payers, the doctors. And so Michael's answer is, 'yes, we will do it.' And we do."

Endnotes

1. Harvard University's Innovations in Government Award.
2. NYT Safety Net Savior by Kevin Sack, May 1, 1992.

Chapter 2

Growing Pains: Building an Integrated Network

"The idea was to build a network that was not a feeder system so much as an organization where people would get the care they needed in the appropriate part of the continuum."

Howard Gold

"What might be possible if we were to pool our resources?"

They were the medical equivalent of the Hatfields and the McCoys. North Shore University Hospital in Manhasset and Long Island Jewish Medical Center in New Hyde Park, a mere ten minutes apart, competed "like rams fighting for turf," in the words of one administrator. Founded a year apart in the 1950s, they expanded over time competing for patients, doctors, benefactors, and money. By the mid and late 1990s, the health care landscape in New York and nationally shifted giving insurance companies the upper hand in many negotiations and squeezing revenues for hospitals and physician groups. With tougher economic times, competition intensified even as the two organizations searched for safe harbors. This was the trend throughout the country—hospitals and doctors' groups eagerly, even frantically in some cases, searching for partners, seeking to be acquired by, or to partner with, large academic medical centers.

Long Island Jewish Medical Center, with a reputation for clinical excellence, was a particular target, and was courted by large, Manhattan-based hospital systems. Marriage would be blissful, was the lure. But what sounded, initially, like something special did not hold up very well upon closer examination. The reality was that the big, brand-name players in Manhattan wanted Long Island hospitals as sources of referrals; as funnels through which to refer patients and cash into Manhattan. It was about sending commercially insured patients—no Medicare and certainly no Medicaid patients, thank you!—into the big city. Hospital leaders saw through the masquerading suitors and turned away, but both Long Island Jewish Medical Center (LIJ) and North Shore University Hospital knew that being out there as an aging single, alone in an unforgiving marketplace, was no way to live.

And then, after discussions with the potential safe harbors in Manhattan broke off, the Hatfields and McCoys decided to do something previously unthinkable—*talk to each other!* But even getting to the point where they sat down together took some thought. A central player throughout all of this was Ralph Nappi, a prominent attorney who had served as a trustee and former chair at North Shore University Hospital as far back as 1972 (and remains on the board 42 years later). Nappi was in the middle of all the negotiations and he credits a number of the administrative leaders for making it happen, including Jack Gallagher, North Shore CEO at the time, but he also emphasizes the critical roles played by the respective Board chairs of the two hospitals, two well-respected New York business leaders and philanthropists. Saul Katz, chair of the board at North Shore University Hospital, was a successful businessman in real estate and co-owner of the New York Mets, while Roy Zuckerberg, chair of the board at Long Island

Jewish, was vice chairman at Goldman Sachs. It seemed clear, at least to these men, that they might be able to build a new entity together.

In the late 1990s, Saul Katz would hold informal gatherings on Saturday mornings to discuss various challenges facing North Shore Hospital. On one particular Saturday morning, Katz looked around at those present—including Ralph Nappi, Jack Gallagher, and Michael Dowling—and, as Nappi recalls it, "he said, 'guys, give me one good reason why we shouldn't merge with LIJ. Don't shoot from hip. I want considered thought.' Katz was emphatic. *Our mission is to serve the community*, he told his colleagues. He challenged the team: *Tell me why the community would not benefit from this? We are a not-for-profit. Our job is to improve the level of care for the entire community.* So he asked us to think it over and come back together to discuss it. We talked about it for several weeks and not one of us could come up with a reason why we shouldn't do it. We said, 'Saul, there is no reason not to merge, but it won't be easy to get them to the table.'" Katz and Roy Zuckerberg, the LIJ Board chair, had a conversation. "We set up a group of five or six people from each hospital and created a negotiating committee," recalls Nappi. "We had a couple of meetings. This wasn't exactly rocket science! It was a no brainer. We felt we could be a major player and do a better job together improving quality."

Jeff Kraut, then an executive at Long Island Jewish, recalls going into the first meeting between the two sides in December in 1996, and looking across the table at Michael Dowling and the team from North Shore. "Mike was the COO then and he and his team got up and talked about the North Shore strategy," recalls Kraut, "and then we got up and talked about the Long Island Jewish Medical Center strategy and, *lo and behold*, they were the same strategy! We're both going to spend 50 million dollars stealing business from each other with no net benefit. So the obvious question was, *what might be possible if we were to pool our resources?*" If not the same strategy, exactly, they were certainly complementary, says Howard Gold. It is fair to say in retrospect that "North Shore was focused on hospitals, Long Island Jewish was focused on doctors," says Gold. "Well, you have to do both. LIJ wanted friendly relationships with the payers since they dictated the rules on how to get paid whereas we at North Shore saw the payers as withholding the payments we earned legitimately by providing service to their members—our patients. We realized both sides of the equation were necessary for success. North Shore was focused on Nassau and Suffolk [counties on Long Island] and Long Island Jewish was focused on the adjacent county of Queens. North Shore was more business focused and LIJ was more clinical focused. North Shore was more corporate and LIJ was more academic. It was clear that a marriage could make sense if we both stretched the boundaries of each other's thinking—and there was some urgency about it given the emerging economics of the health care marketplace."

Just a year earlier, New York State had deregulated hospital rates which sent revenues downward. These declines came as reimbursements from Medicare also dropped and as insurance companies were gaining ability to drive down prices they were willing to pay hospitals and physician groups for most services. At the time, the Long Island Jewish organization included three hospitals, while the North Shore system included ten. Financially, North Shore was a much stronger organization than Long Island Jewish in large measure due to the leadership team that had guided North Shore through the challenges of the 1990s. Jack Gallagher, Ralph Nappi and Saul Katz were ahead of their time building the first true health care *system* in New York state. "Jack and Ralph had a concept about creating a health system," says Dowling. "Nobody was doing it back then. North Shore was way ahead of everybody else." Gallagher, Nappi, and former North Shore University Hospital board chair Robert Kaufman had assembled a North Shore network of ten hospitals *prior to the merger* with Long Island Jewish.

One aspect of their strategy was to merge with community hospitals, many of which were in financial trouble. The acquisition costs were relatively low and those investments enabled the building of the network. When Dowling joined North Shore in 1995 as Chief Operating Officer he worked with Gallagher and Nappi to continue the acquisition strategy. Gallagher and Nappi had a vision for a broader health care delivery network similar to what Dowling had been advocating in the Cuomo Administration. When he arrived from Albany, Dowling pushed to build a network not just of community hospitals but one including tertiary care, physician groups, specialty care, nursing homes, end-of-life care; a network capable of fulfilling any health care need a patient in any stage of life might require; a network that would serve every health need within their communities. There was no such organization in the state of New York at the time. "When Michael was in the governor's office he wanted to build networks instead of independent hospitals," says Howard Gold. "All along, the idea was to build networks of providers and work in tandem with managed care companies."

At the time of the merger North Shore faced financial challenges but Long Island Jewish was confronted with an unsettling financial picture, due in some sense to management and governance issues. The board went beyond its traditional policy role—so much so that the joke at the time was that *the board was so involved in operations they'd go into the kitchen and taste the soup before it was served.* While North Shore had been steadily expanding its facilities in the 1990s, Long Island Jewish was deferring maintenance and investing little money in the operation. After a series of discussions, the two organizations reached a deal to join forces. Many of the specifics were left to be worked out later, but there was a binding legal agreement to merge. Right from the start, however, there was a formidable obstacle: The United States Department of Justice opposed the merger—adamantly so. Historically, in similar cases, few hospital systems fought against federal opposition.

The deck was stacked in favor of the government in most cases, but the teams from North Shore and Long Island Jewish believed they had a case to make. During a two week trial in August of 1997, Justice Department attorneys argued that the merger would reduce competition in the marketplace, but most of the witnesses at trial contradicted that assertion. The cause received an important boost when the New York state attorney general stated that the merger would not only "not impair competition," but that it was "in the best interest of the State and its citizens."

In announcing a victory for the North Shore–Long Island Jewish team versus the government, the court found that the Justice Department "failed to prove that the merger of these hospitals will substantially lessen competition, increase hospital prices above competitive level or in any way reduce services at the merged entity." This was a decisive victory and one in which the court indicated a clear understanding of the marketplace forces at work in health care. The judge stated in the ruling that "there were many catalysts producing this merger, including the rapidly evolving and changing conditions in the present health care market, increasingly empty hospital beds, the managed care phenomena, competitive bidding caused by deregulation and reduced Government spending on Medicare and Medicaid."

It was a huge win for the newly merged entity, but it was obvious right away that this was one of those marriages where the fighting starts en route to the honeymoon.

Culture Clash

Any thought that the court case meant the end of conflict was sheer fantasy. During the course of the litigation the teams from North Shore and LIJ bonded together against a common enemy, but the ink on the court ruling was barely dry before infighting escalated. Actually, infighting is too mild a term to characterize the rancorous nature of the post-merger relationship. "When the merger was approved everybody started fighting," says Jeff Kraut. "And the fighting reflected the different cultures. At North Shore they might stab you in the back but at Long Island Jewish they would stab you in the chest. Nothing personal!" In these "merger wars," as they were called, scores of people were fighting for a limited number of jobs. The most awkward result of the merger was that there were two people in the new organization for virtually every job and the jockeying for position became intense. The conflict was fierce enough to draw the attention of *The New York Times* which quoted a physician, Dr. Martin Edelstein, about the merger challenge: "These were two independent, historically very competitive medical centers, each with its own department heads and teaching programs, different medical school affiliations and a totally different culture. North Shore had no unions, Long Island Jewish had unions. Each had its own set of trustees and administrators. And they wanted to meld all of this together in the face of shrinking insurance reimbursements and the added burdens of managed care. It's really an incredible task."

The newly joined entity was governed initially by a painfully awkward Noah's Ark structure with co-CEO's, co-COO's, co-everything on down the management line; a structure so unwieldy that it fostered an atmosphere of mistrust and suspicion. After joining forces—at least on paper—the two organizations were more fiercely competitive than ever. "The two hospitals started to compete over everything," says Dennis Dowling, who was running North Shore Hospital at the time. Another person was running Long Island Jewish "and we would both angle to get resources to grow and develop our own institution's services. We competed for new equipment, marketing dollars, facility improvements, everything. There was very little coordination and a lot of competition and this went on for a couple of years."

It was a nightmarish time. "The year or so after the merger was the most our values were challenged," recalls Mark

Solazzo, now Chief Operating Officer at Northwell. "The two merging organizations did not share the same values." Solazzo was clear on this issue. At Long Island Jewish, he says, there was a culture where "people were focused on their own personal agenda and moving that forward and that just wasn't us. At North Shore, the values were a powerful presence." This was not to suggest that the Dowling team was anything less than competitive in the fight over jobs at the new entity, but they were also driven by a mission to create something for the broader community and this was lacking among some leaders at LIJ. The nasty, sustained post-merger conflict, says Solazzo, set the organization back. "We lost two years during that time," he says. "We would be two years ahead of where we are now if we had not had to go through the conflict." Underneath all of the conflict, however, were thousands of employees—nurses, lab workers, technicians, pharmacists, and many others—who were devoted first and foremost to serving patients and worried little, if at all, about the conflict at the more senior levels of the organization. These professionals were not thinking *I am a North Shore person* or *I am an LIJ person*. They were focused on doing good work for patients.

After two bruising years, things settled down and the new health system was able to move forward with an aligned leadership team in place (most of the leadership positions having been won by people from North Shore). This period of peace was significant enough that *The New York Times* took note. "After Merger's Bumpy Start, North Shore–L.I.J. Is Clicking" said the headline in December of 2000. The article, which noted that the two organizations "appear to have made a successful match," quoted Michael Dowling saying that, "there were some potholes in the beginning. But that is to be expected when you bring together two different cultures, two large teaching campuses. The question is, how do you manage it? We have managed it better than most. It is so integrated at this moment that it would be difficult to undo it." The article noted that "independent observers have given the merger high marks" including an official at the state health department who said the merger "improved the financial stability of the health care network and has strengthened its ability to provide quality care to its patients." The *Times* quoted several officials—who clearly were not inside either organization—indicating that "given the circumstances, the merger went remarkably smoothly." The reality was that in 1998, the year after the merger, the system lost tens of millions of dollars in part because such a significant infusion of cash into Long Island Jewish was required. But the marketplace standing of the new entity was evident just two years later in 2000 when, after renegotiating insurance contracts the system turned things around financially and ended the year with a surplus of $25 million.

Dr. Lawrence Smith, Physician-in-Chief at Northwell, was working at Mount Sinai in New York when the merger was happening and had the view of a neutral outsider in what was a fierce partisan battle. "In some ways it was a merger of equals because they both had strengths," says Smith. "North Shore University Hospital had very much started as a community hospital on the Gold Coast of Long Island and grew into an important tertiary facility. They had lots of efficient care and were economically strong. Long Island Jewish Hospital was very much an academic medical center in the tradition of Jewish philanthropic hospitals. There was a lot of emphasis on research, with labs on campus and researchers were encouraged to publish widely. In the world of academic medicine, Long Island Jewish was far better known than North Shore Hospital. North Shore saw this as a very important move to solidify their position in the Long Island marketplace, while Long Island Jewish was looking at it much for the purpose of surviving. They were so different in so many ways that the ability to actually merge them and make them function as one organization is something that is rare in health care in America these days."

Mosaic

From his perspective as Chief Operating Officer, Dowling viewed the system, which at the time included 13 hospitals, as a mosaic. Jeff Kraut channeled Dowling's thinking when he wrote that the system was a "collection of organizations each with their own individual history, culture and personality, that are bound together by a common set of beliefs, goals and values. The System, like a mosaic, is comprised of unique and interesting individual pieces, but when placed side-by-side, the whole is more impressive than any one piece. Operationalizing this concept means working together, building trust, respecting each other's views, getting input from all sources and recognizing that good ideas can emanate from any location. It is about respecting our uniqueness and mutuality of purpose."

When Dowling succeeded Jack Gallagher as CEO, this description of the mosaic was more aspirational than real. The hospitals within the system, large and small, were quite different in many ways and while some shared "beliefs, goals, and values," others differed. Certainly there was no unified culture that defined the new organization. Mark Solazzo recalls many times when the leadership team was flying forward without an entirely clear vision of what lay ahead. "We had an idea to build a network, but we had no plan," he says. "We took so many risks trying to figure it out; risks at times when we had no more than twenty days cash on hand! And still we were acquiring these hospitals, many of them with weak balance sheets and we would struggle to integrate them. We were figuring it out as we went along." More than anything else during the first three years after the merger, says Solazzo, the leadership worked to define and build "a team-based, collaborative culture one interaction at a time, one meeting at a time, one acquisition at a time."

There had been some good lessons learned about how not to bring new hospitals into the system and the lessons were reflected in Dowling's mosaic concept. Hospitals with deep roots in communities tend to have distinctive cultures and that often makes integrating hospitals into a large system a challenge. Northwell learned the hard way *how not to do it.* Back in 1990, the first foray into attempting to build a system came when North Shore acquired Glen Cove Hospital on Long Island. "For the first year or two we completely screwed it up," recalls Dennis Dowling. "We thought a lot of ourselves as an administration and we drove over to Glen Cove and we were going to show the local country bumpkins. We were going to take over. There was resentment and pushback and we found out that our show at North Shore, as good as it was, didn't travel well. We learned. I guess it's business 101 but we learned that we needed to move in a more collegial, coopera-tive manner, rather than like a bulldozer. It took us a couple of years to sort it out but we learned from it."

The lesson would prove crucial in subsequent efforts at acquisitions. Some years later Northwell was seeking to acquire a community hospital that was also being pursued by a major Manhattan-based hospital. The competitor came in from Manhattan and made clear to the community hospital that they would control everything from Manhattan starting day one. There was little, if any, diplomatic effort made. All of the signage, for example, was changed suddenly, which may not seem significant except that it makes for a radical identity change virtually overnight. This was profoundly uncomfortable for the staff, trustees and patients at the community hospital and they pushed back enough to get out of the deal and part-ner with Northwell, whose team comes in and reaffirms that the name of the community hospital would not ever change.

"'We are not going to change the brand,' we told them," recalls Ralph Nappi. "'We are going to *enhance* it.' They felt burned by the New York City suitors and they were still sus-picious when we came in. When they asked us questions, we gave them answers, we gave them reasons, explained the factors behind any decision that affected them, we brought the chairman of the Northwell Board to talk with them and listen to them. We say, 'here is what we think makes sense, what we think should happen.' We do not go in and say, 'this is the way it's going to be!' "

Dowling wrote in a strategic plan that Northwell "does not create a distinction in the structure of its operations between tertiary and community hospitals. Community hospitals are not viewed as a spoke of a tertiary hub …" From the start, Gallagher and Dowling worked to create a unified network where the various entities retained their individual characteristics but where the aspiration, and eventual reality, was toward a common culture and an integrated entity where core elements—finance, IT, contracting, administration—were woven together and where the overall entity adapted to the addition of new hospitals and physician groups. "The goal was not just to acquire but to integrate all the pieces," says Gold. "Nothing sits out there on the side, everything is working together." This was, and remains, a crucial point of differentiation between Northwell and some of the large brand name hospitals in Manhattan. Dowling wanted the collection of hospitals to "act like a system." This held many meanings including identifying quality protocols and standardizing them throughout the system where appropriate. It also meant working as one—a unified entity dealing with insurance companies—crucial for the long-term success of the organization. Dowling had been thinking about this approach while still up in Albany. "The idea we talked about in Albany was to build a network that was not a feeder system so much as an organization where people would get the care they needed in the appropriate part of the continuum," says Gold. "We believed all along in setting up provider networks with primary care doctors as a central piece and hospitals were really big and very often when we were in Albany we were considered anti-hospital because we wanted money from the hospitals to build ambulatory and primary care. We thought patients could be taken care of by primary care teams and specialists who would coordinate the care depending upon the individual needs of each patient."

Level Playing Field

To be able to build an integrated delivery network required standing in the marketplace. "We wanted the payers to deal with us on a level playing field," says Gold. Early on, insurance companies "came in and said, 'we are going to take your business away unless you give us a price reduction.' And Jack Gallagher and Michael, who was then chief operating officer, aspired to mutual interdependence not domination by either side. Before this, managed care payers dominated the marketplace. Their intent was then, as it is now, to pick apart each provider and negotiate with individual doctors, separately with each hospital, home care services, as separate fragmented entities. They would pit one provider group against another. And we said we would work as a system. We were a fully integrated system at the corporate and clinical levels. And we presented a unified, integrated system to payers to create mutual interdependence and equivalence with them in the marketplace. We wanted a transaction among equals."

Dowling knew financial success was a prerequisite to achieving his goals. From the start, he aspired to achieve an A rating financially. One of the curious things about the early days of the network when Dowling took over was that he had spent virtually his entire professional life in academia or government. Strictly speaking, his experience in business had been at Blue Cross and lasted just seven months. But from the start Dowling was acutely aware of the need to base all of his aspirations on a foundation of financial success. Unless the system was healthy financially nothing else would work; nothing else was possible. His aspiration to achieve an A credit rating indicated his level of commitment to financial health. The rating, a Wall Street measure of success, required a certain level of debt as well as a certain level of cash on hand and it was this series of requirements to achieve an A rating that left even some insiders at Northwell skeptical.

"People from a major investment house and hedge fund were on our board," says Jeff Kraut, "and they were saying, 'never going to happen. Are you crazy? You have no idea. You can't do that.' When you say you want to be A rated it's very clear you got to get cash, you got to make a margin, you got to save money and you got to invest. Now the concept of A rated was never discussed because up until that time we went into the debt market, we went into FHA insured money. We never went into the market and that was the plan on how we were going to finance ourselves."

The drive for an A rating was an indication that Dowling's ambitions went beyond what Northwell had done before. Dowling was ambitious. He sought to create the first corporate university within a health care organization in the U.S. modeled on the corporate university at GE; to build a new medical school from scratch; to create the largest private emergency response system anywhere in health care; to start a new insurance company; to deal with payers on an integrated basis and start to offer less expensive insurance products to consumers who would access Northwell health care services primarily; and to step into the poorest communities in the New York area to save hospitals and doctor practices and, not only improve the health of the community, but boost the economy and living conditions as well. And, oh yes, he wanted to grow beyond the New York area to New Jersey and Connecticut and the truth was that he aspired to build a health care organization from Boston to Washington, D.C.

Chapter 3

Learning Obsession

"How can you be a great organization without investing in people and lifelong learning?"

Jeff Kraut

"Learning organizations will lead the pack in this new era."

At John F. Kennedy International Airport, a month before he was to take over as CEO of Northwell Health, Michael Dowling boarded a flight for Seattle, where he was scheduled to speak at a conference. He would not normally welcome six hours in the air but on this evening Dowling had a lot on his mind and wanted to get it down on paper. He was thinking about the future of the organization and, as he did so, he kept coming back to his lifelong interest in learning. This interest bordering on obsession was an essential strand within Dowling's DNA. Since first arriving at Northwell, he had been exploring the possibility of creating an internal learning organization. "When he got here he had the germ of that concept and he had had people working on putting some ideas on paper," says Mark Solazzo. "He was pushing, and testing and thinking about how to do it." He had recently conducted an informal inventory of the "training programs" within Northwell and had come away concerned. "If you want to go from here to there you have to think about what will be needed in the future and then train people—not train them for the world that *is*, which is what most places do, but train them, educate them for what lies ahead," he says. "When I was at Fordham University some of the professors had notepads with lectures that were moldy because they were the same old lectures they gave in the 1950s. No thought process about going forward just regurgitating the same old BS over and over and over again. When I came to North Shore I remember sitting with HR in the beginning and I said, 'well tell me a little bit about your training programs,' and I got this inventory of the number of people that went through training classes. I said, 'what is the organizing theme? What are we doing?' It was all over the place. I said, 'what is the benefit of it all? I know what the cost is. What is the *benefit*?'" The organizing theme? There didn't seem to be one. The benefit? Unclear.

As his flight headed west, Dowling began writing out his thoughts. "Over the past decade a transformation, as subtle as an earthquake, has affected the healthcare industry," he wrote. "As with most earthquakes, a new landscape has begun to emerge. The powerful forces of change are multifactorial and include: a shift in social demographic characteristics, the development of revolutionary medical technology, consumer demand for high quality, low cost healthcare, and a change in medical delivery models and organizational structures ..." How to deal with the aftershocks of this earthquake? Nothing could have been more obvious to Dowling: *You learn your way through*. Education had been a force powerful enough to transport him from the poverty of Limerick to the leadership of one of the nation's leading health systems. He knew people wanted something more than a job that produced income. They wanted the kind of personal fulfillment that came with rewarding work; work you cared about. What mattered was doing something that mattered and doing it well. Yes, there was a certain amount of drudgery to almost any work and, from experience, Dowling knew drudgery. But he knew as well the joyful side of work and he knew it came not in a role where you were instructed to do x, y and z. Rather, fulfillment in work came in a job that was challenging and demanding; a job in which you were provided with the tools needed to grow and improve. To Dowling, education lay at the heart of this. The key to fulfilling work—not just at the start of a career but every day throughout a lifetime—was learning. As he flew to Seattle, his thoughts crystallized. He wanted to build the best learning center ever seen at a health care organization. He didn't know *exactly* what it would look like or even *generally* what it would look like but he knew that continuous learning had the power to lift individuals and the organization.

Health care is mind-numbingly complex at some levels and it was unreasonable to expect that people would somehow figure it out on their own. How could you expect excellence in an incredibly complex, rapidly changing industry, unless you defined and aspired to excellence through learning and innovation? The answer, Dowling believed, lay in the notion of *continuous learning by every employee at all levels sustained over a lifetime.* Under Dowling's thinking it would not be possible to graduate from the learning venture within Northwell. It would never end. More than that, there would be a learning cycle where, over time, a person would serve as a faculty member one day, student the next.

"Learning organizations will lead the pack in this new era," he wrote, noting that it was important for organizations to "foster and facilitate personal growth and lifelong learning among its employees. This is the hallmark of a learning organization …" As Dowling looked around at companies he admired—especially outside the health care space—he saw that "other industries have already experienced the change in landscape [health care was undergoing] and have addressed these same issues that we face today. Learning from their experiences will aid us in creating an institute that is not only unique but one that advances the profound organizational culture change that is necessary. This institute is not a 'training program.' It will be the driving force which transforms [Northwell] into a learning organization" that develops "a cadre of leaders at all levels throughout the organization."

Dowling was familiar with learning programs at major companies including IBM and Motorola, and he had had a particular attraction to GE, where lifelong learning was at the core of the company's values, as evidenced by the company spending nearly a billion dollars annually on its educational programs. GE was a pioneer. As far back as 1956 the company established a learning center at Crotonville, a bucolic setting north of New York City. In the more than half century since its founding, Crotonville had become synonymous with excellence in corporate leadership education. The ultimate goal of the company, of course, was profitability, but GE leaders recognized that personal growth and development of its workers—particularly its leaders—were essential to financial success. The Crotonville educational approach aimed to help employees maximize their individual strengths and to set out on a journey that would elevate a career from a job to a meaningful life experience. Dowling liked that idea very much. That is what he wanted for his employees—the kind of education that would help them perform at the highest level to the benefit of the organization and to their own personal fulfillment. Dowling wanted the work people did at Northwell to bring meaning that comes when one is engaged in something that matters; a venture where the goal is in some way the betterment of life for people. For Dowling, of course, this was a continuation of his time working with Mario Cuomo. The setting was now different, most of the people were different, but the mission remained the same.

Dowling knew Jeff Immelt, the CEO at GE, and he thought that Immelt and his team at Crotonville would be ideal tutors to get Dowling and his team started. Dowling saw GE as a key piece of the puzzle but he felt that wasn't enough. He wanted another partner from academia and he sought out David

Shore, one of the deans at the Harvard T.H. Chan School of
Public Health. Both Immelt and Shore agreed to help. On his
flight to Seattle, Dowling wrote that the partnership to create
a new learning entity at Northwell would "combine the best
of three elements: the experience and expertise of the private
for-profit sector (GE); the expertise from the best of academia
(Harvard); and the expertise and experience of a large, successful health provider network (Northwell)."

"This is a wonderful thing. There was no thing."

Like Dowling, Kathleen Gallo was obsessed with education. She grew up in Queens where she attended Catholic
grammar and high school, and then completed a 12 month
program and received a Licensed Practical Nurse degree and
went to work at the Hospital for Special Surgery in Manhattan,
where she modeled herself on the older, more experienced
nurses. "I was on the top floor with nurses who were such
good role models I wanted to be just like them," she says. "I
had white shoe polish and would shine my shoes every night
and I bleached my shoelaces because I wanted to be spotless."
She then earned a degree as a Registered Nurse and knew she
found her calling. "I absolutely loved it, loved nursing school,
loved the work, loved doing clinical," she says. But as an RN
she wanted to learn more and she left the Hospital for Special
Surgery, a cushy assignment as these things go, and applied
for a position at one of New York City's public hospitals,
Elmhurst General, where there was a diverse and often challenging patient mix (including a women's prison unit). When
she applied for the job at Elmhurst the director of nursing
interviewing her asked incredulously: "You left Special Surgery
to work *here?*" Gallo asked to be put into the float pool, not
generally a popular assignment, because she wanted to learn
about many different areas within the hospital.

After her sons were born in 1979 and 1980, Gallo took
some time off, but by 1981 was back to work every other
weekend at North Shore University Hospital Emergency

Department. Several years later, when the boys reached grammar school age, she was back on an educational track. "I would put the boys on a school bus in the morning then go take classes at Stony Brook toward my masters and then meet them at the bus at 3 o'clock," she recalls. "My goal was to get my education so by the time my boys were in high school I would have everything in my back pocket and I could go back to work." While pursuing her degree she worked nursing shifts every other weekend at the North Shore emergency department. She would take additional overnight shifts here and there but had to be home by 6 a.m. when her husband headed out to his job. As she neared completing work for a master's degree at Stony Brook University, Gallo accepted an opportunity to teach a nursing course at Stony Brook, where the Dean encouraged her to pursue a doctorate. She did so, enrolling in a nursing PhD program at Adelphi University in Garden City, Long Island. She completed her coursework and then settled upon a dissertation topic: "A philosophical inquiry based on theories of justice into the moral obligation for state government to have designated trauma centers." This was interesting in its own right, certainly a topic worth exploring, but it also serves as a clue to Gallo's sense of mission that aligns with Dowling's and others at Northwell. Gallo did something else a bit unusual in her coursework. While most of her colleagues in the program chose history of nursing or something similar as their elective option, Gallo took a course in economics. She found the "dismal science," as philosopher Thomas Carlyle termed economics, to be anything but. So compelling did she find the subject matter, in fact, that she plunged into an MBA program just as she was completing her PhD. In 1996, a year after earning an MBA, and with her boys now in high school, she was recruited back to Northwell by the chair of emergency medicine to work as his administrative partner organizing emergency medicine across the system. It was in this role that Dowling took note of her work.

Dowling was scheduled to take over as Northwell CEO on January 1, 2002. Prior to that, he laid out a plan and he asked Gallo whether she would be willing to take on a new role within the organization; in fact, a new role in health care—that of Chief Learning Officer. It would be something special, Dowling told her—the first internal corporate university in health care. Major industrial and service companies included chief learning officers among their executives, but health care lagged in this area. Now Northwell would follow in the steps of organizations such as IBM and General Electric. Gallo accepted the position and, just about a month later, Dowling asked her to take on leadership of HR, as well.

On January 15, 2002, Dowling held a press conference at the InterContinental Hotel in Manhattan announcing the creation of the Center for Learning and Innovation within the health system. "So we held a press conference," Dowling recalls, "and I stood up and I had Jeffrey Immelt with me and I had David Shore [from Harvard] and I announced this wonderful thing. Jeff stood up and says, 'this is a wonderful thing.' David Shore says, 'this is a wonderful thing.' *There was no thing.*" He told Gallo they had to move fast to build it and, as Dowling put it, "with Kathy, you don't have to tell her more than once." The new enterprise began modestly enough with a pilot program aimed at a hand-selected group of middle managers. The curriculum included basics of finance, HR, quality, and leadership, and was taught by a faculty comprised of Northwell senior executives, "leader as teacher," as Gallo put it. Gallo knew the executive team was deeply familiar with the material and she also knew that if senior execs taught the courses people would actually show up for class.

Gallo and her team built the curriculum with the guidance of the GE consultants from Crotonville and some faculty from the Harvard School of Public Health. "We relied on them to make sure that we were building something academically sound," says Gallo. "We wanted to make sure we had the right principles." She was guided, as well, by her own readings into the work of MIT faculty member Peter Senge, author of the landmark book *The Fifth Discipline: The Art and Practice of the Learning Organization*. Senge's work defined some of the thinking from Dowling and Gallo particularly as it related to the power of meaning in work and the importance of learning within a professional setting. "When you ask people about what it is like being part of a great team, what is most striking is the meaningfulness of the experience," Senge writes in *The Fifth Discipline*. "People talk about being part of something larger than themselves ..." Gallo was drawn to Senge's definition of mastery and the need to pursue it within an educational setting. "People with a high level of personal mastery live in a continual learning mode," he wrote. "They never 'arrive' ... personal mastery is not something you possess. It is a process. It is a lifelong discipline ..."

The other early initiative from Gallo involved teaching certain employees to think differently about quality and management and she did this by introducing a lean Six Sigma management methodology. Six Sigma is defined as "a disciplined, data-driven approach and methodology for eliminating defects (driving toward six standard deviations between the mean and the nearest specification limit) in any process—from manufacturing to transactional and from product to service."[1] Jack Welch, the former CEO at GE described Six Sigma as "a quality program that, when all is said and done, improves your customer's experience, lowers your costs, and builds better leaders." Gallo had been hearing about Six Sigma for years from her brother, president of a division at Ford Motor Company. She asked him to come in and teach some of the basics of the approach to the administrative team in the emergency services department, which was struggling with a variety of problems including inefficient billing. With some additional training the team was able to streamline the billing process, reducing mistakes (defects in the Six Sigma parlance), and improving revenues. Just as importantly, the process of learning the Six Sigma approach expanded the thinking of the administrative team. They became more open to change and much more aware of using data to identify waste and inefficiencies.

"Nobody in health care was using Six Sigma at the time, but with health care being so process rich it made perfect sense," says Gallo. As other organizations have since discovered, implementing Six Sigma or the Toyota Production System lean management approach in a health care setting is fraught with challenges. "We had our first report out with these teams," says Gallo, "because we wanted to show their success, and their courage for being the first pioneers, and we called it the CEOs report out to build in some accountability for leadership, that really perhaps did not think it was a very valuable process. Mike said, 'I want people to start thinking differently.' We wanted to be able to identify opportunities for improvement, having a disciplined methodology to use with support around them. And Mike will tell you, it was a bumpy road. It took some time for people to accept that we could learn from other industries. Now it is pretty much embedded in the organization. It does not have to be watched over. I watched over it and kept it very close to me like I was bringing a two-year old to an amusement park. Because it could very easily have disappeared."

Learning from Top Gun

Gallo's pursuit of learning paid off in an important way in 2004 when she traveled to a conference for HR executives and chief learning officers from various industries. During the course of the meeting Gallo found herself sitting next to Michael Barger from JetBlue Airways and they struck up a conversation. Barger served as the Chief Learning Officer at JetBlue University, the learning center training crew members.

Barger had earned a PhD in Education at the University of Pennsylvania and been commissioned as an officer in the United States Navy. He flew the F/A-18 Hornet fighter jet during the Gulf War. In all, he served three deployments flying from aircraft carriers the USS Theodore Roosevelt and the USS Dwight David Eisenhower. Barger's expertise went beyond serving as a fighter pilot. He was also a teacher working for a time as Chief Instructor at the Navy Fighter Weapons School where the elite of the elites in the U.S. did their training. This was the school known as TOPGUN made famous in the Tom Cruise movie. In addition to these credentials, Barger had been among the founders of JetBlue in 1999 where he served as senior leader responsible for all flight and maintenance operations. Gallo and Barger hit it off and the more they talked that day, the clearer it became that they had something in common that set them apart from their colleagues at the conference. Chief learning officers at American Express or Xerox faced challenging issues, no doubt. But in their jobs, Gallo and Barger, faced challenges an order of magnitude greater for the reality in health care and air travel was that lives were at stake every minute of every day.

Barger told Gallo about Crew Resource Management. This was the approach that had been adopted by major airlines throughout the world after the worst crash in aviation history. In March of 1977, a KLM 747 took off from the island of Tenerife, part of Spain's Canary Islands. The KLM jet crashed into a Pan American 747 occupying the same runway. In dense fog, the crew of the KLM jet believed, incorrectly, that they had clearance from air traffic control to take off. Reaching a speed of 160 miles per hour, the jet began to take off just as a crew member spotted the other plane directly in front of it. As the KLM jet lifted off its engines and landing gear struck the Pan Am plane and its huge fuel tanks were ignited. In all, 583 passengers and crew aboard the two planes were killed. On the Pan Am plane, miraculously, 61 people survived.

After the crash, air safety experts gathered to study what had gone wrong. They identified many problems, including poor communication between the planes and air traffic control as well as miscommunication among crew members. Industry leaders put their cultures under a microscope and found significant flaws. Among the greatest was a culture in which crew members never questioned a captain; where one person made all relevant judgments without full benefit of the highly trained and capable other members of the crew. "This hierarchy is deadly in an airplane or an operating room," says Gallo. "Everybody's input should be welcome. Crew Resource Management is essentially about collapsing the hierarchy gradient that occurs in the cockpit in a way that fosters free-flowing communication." The consultancy Safer Healthcare notes that "Crew Resource Management in healthcare is concerned not so much with the technical knowledge and skills required to operate equipment or perform specific operations, but rather with the cognitive and interpersonal skills needed to effectively manage a team-based, high-risk activity.[2]"

The Power of Simulation

Barger told Gallo how pilots and other crew members trained in teams and sought to flatten the power gradient by using various invented scenarios to test and train the crews. Gallo asked him how he trained fighter pilots. "Simulation," he replied, explaining that with sophisticated cockpit simulation the Navy was able to put pilots through a wide array of challenges before ever leaving the ground. While simulation was a way of life in the Navy in particular and aeronautics in general, it had yet to penetrate the world of patient safety in health care.

Gallo went back to Northwell and began digging into the use of simulation in health care. She found that the relatively recent yet extensive use of simulation in anesthesiology had improved safety and she was drawn to the idea that simulation might somehow be used more broadly to improve safety in the delivery of care. Like most leaders in health care in the United States, she had been struck by the report from the Institute of Medicine of the National Academies (1999) indicating that as many as 100,000 Americans died each year from avoidable medical mistakes. It was believed that many of these deaths were due to lack of teamwork and communication, and it was in this area that Barger made an important connection for Gallo. He told her about Robert L. Helmreich, PhD, who worked for many years developing safety in the airlines and who had turned his attention to doing the same within health care. Helmreich, trained in psychology, was something of a legend. He was widely acknowledged as the father of Crew Resource Management and one of the leading thinkers in the field of human factors psychology. In 2004, Gallo, along with her Northwell colleague, Gene Tangney, traveled to Texas to meet with Helmreich. Like Barger, he was gracious and thoughtful in his discussions about safety. He talked about aspiring to a culture of safety where any team member, upon seeing something dangerous, would be entirely free to speak up. In aviation the saying was "anybody can ground the flight." Helmreich believed the same should be true in health care. The more Gallo talked with Barger and Helmreich, and the more she read into safety literature, the stronger her belief that there were rich lessons for health care in the fields of aviation and in the military. Think about the complexity involved in aviation and in naval operations on nuclear-powered submarines and aircraft carriers. "There is a reason you don't hear about many accidents in those places," she says.

Helmreich's thinking was influential in the creation of Team STEPPS (Team Strategies and Tools to Enhance Performance and Patient Safety), a Crew Resource Management approach to health care. "Team STEPPS is a teamwork system developed jointly by the Department of Defense and the Agency for Healthcare Research and Quality (AHRQ) to improve institutional collaboration and communication relating to patient safety."[3] Team STEPPS has become pervasive throughout health care in the United States, and in many areas of Northwell. It is defined by AHRQ as "an evidence-based set of teamwork tools, aimed at optimizing patient outcomes by improving communication and teamwork skills among health care professionals. It includes a comprehensive set of ready-to-use materials and a training curriculum to successfully integrate teamwork principles into any health care system." This same federal agency has emphasized that "simulation has proven to be a powerful strategy in team-based health care. It affords excellent opportunities to enhance the quality of continuing education for health care professionals, as well as provide education and practice for students learning to become health care professionals."[4]

Gallo learned a good deal about the potential applications of simulation in health care from Helmreich as well as through visits to simulation centers at the University of Pittsburgh School of Medicine and elsewhere. She also absorbed the latest report from the Institute of Medicine, *A Bridge to Quality*, focused on education in the health professions, which "emphasized the need for a substantial shift in educational strategy and methodology, replacing the older model of professional autonomy with one that emphasized teamwork and interprofessional learning. The aim, to improve safety, was in full alignment with the theory underlying clinical simulation ..."

Building a learning center such as CLI was, in itself, a learning journey. At each step along the way, in pursuit of outside experts, Gallo traveled to whatever companies, think-tanks, or universities she believed might be helpful. As she toured simulation centers at the University of Miami, Hartford Hospital, and elsewhere, she had basic questions in mind: What, exactly, does a simulation center look like? What equipment and infrastructure is needed? Who are the instructors and what do they do? By the end of 2004 she was convinced that simulation could be an important element within the CLI curriculum and, in particular, that it could play a role in patient safety. After her due diligence Gallo purchased a Laerdle high fidelity simulator for about $40,000 and installed it in what was to be the new Northwell sim center in Hauppauge, Long Island, a 5000 square foot facility about 25 miles from the Northwell corporate offices.

"I have never flown a plane but I did graduate number one in my class so I am sure everything will be fine. Please 'buckle up'."

The more Gallo examined the world of simulation the more convinced she grew that it could make a difference in quality and safety. "We know that bringing a lot of people into a big room and lecturing to them for hours on end does nothing but demonstrate that the person in the front of the room is reinforcing his or her own knowledge," she says. "And while that person can leave and check the box that they taught that day, they cannot check the box and say with certainty that anybody *learned* that day. You need learner engagement right from the get go. If you were getting on a plane to go on vacation and the pilot said, 'well, I just want to let everybody know you're in good hands. I attended every lecture that they gave and I earned a hundred on every test. I have never flown a plane but I did graduate number one in my class so I am sure everything will be fine. Please buckle up'."

Activity-based learning, says Gallo, learning where clinicians or students are working on a patient with a particular set of symptoms, for example, creates a certain amount of stress that is appropriate for the occasion and concentrates the learner's mind. This is the kind of engagement from which people learn well, she says. The high fidelity simulator was a plastic body connected to a computer capable of creating a variety of symptoms within the body. For example, the simulator as patient could talk and respond to questions. This was done via a staff member from the sim center in the control room. The simulated body was capable of having any heart rate, blood pressure, or pulse. In fact, almost any sort of challenging situation, including high-risk, rare events could be replicated in the simulation center. And as demonstrated in other simulation centers, Gallo saw how simulated events could effectively create the "suspension of disbelief" essential to effective learning. While all the participants know very well that the "patient" in the bed is a plastic creation linked to computers, the simulation literature notes that during the simulation process, a suspension of disbelief takes places among both students and experienced clinicians. This, in turn, creates an appropriate and realistic level of stress and enhances the learning process.

Courses at CLI emerge from the grass roots—from physicians or nurses in one of the many Northwell hospitals or clinics who feel the need for quality improvement in a particular area. "We develop programs based on the population that asks for it," says Gallo. When someone comes to CLI with an idea, the staff, led by Robert Kerner, who manages the center day-to-day, meets with them, explains the CLI capabilities, and then the person goes back and develops a program description. What is it exactly that the program should accomplish? What are the challenges the clinical team faces? What is the problem to be solved? The team seeking help from CLI puts a program description together with clear objectives. "The program description does not have to be perfect but it does tell us how serious the person is," says Gallo. When someone comes back to CLI with a solid idea—a safety program for a surgical team, for example—CLI staff help identify which surgical team members should be involved. A commitment by staff members to participate in the program is taken seriously at CLI. As Gallo ruefully puts it: "You need to identify which of your team members will be coming to the sessions and they have to show up. Nobody can drop their staff off and come back and pick them up later. This not daycare, nor do we have exorcists on the team who can change your staff so we send them back to you as different people." Simulation programs are generally developed by teams rather than by any single individual. Faculty members at CLI work with leaders from throughout the health system to create instructional simulation lab scenarios. There is an art to creating these scenarios and several of Gallo's team members traveled to Harvard and took the simulation faculty development program there on how to create simulation scenarios and, even more importantly, how to debrief the team members after the sim sessions have been run.

Once the curriculum is set, the CLI team established a schedule that is locked in. "You can't come once," says Gallo. "You waste your time and our time if you're going to come once, so it's either every week, twice a month, once a month, or quarterly. In and out does not serve anybody. It is like going to baseball practice once. Athletic teams practice more than they play the game." Initially, Gallo says, she and her colleagues were focused on the sim machine itself. "For the first two years we thought it was all about the high fidelity simulator," she recalls. "Then, as we learned and matured, we became involved with the Society for Simulation in Healthcare and we realized the simulator is just a tool and it is really all about the learning methodology that you surround it with. You want to provide an appropriate level of stress to keep everybody engaged but at the same time we make sure that it is a safe learning environment;" that is, an environment where anyone can make a mistake without fear; where the session is about learning and improvement rather than judgment. Psychological safety is essential for learning to occur.

From the start, Gallo had all simulation sessions recorded both with video and audio. She learned from other industries, she says, that "the most important thing is after simulation, people sit down and go through a debriefing and the debriefing is much longer than the simulation, because that's where everybody learns." How, she wondered, were the most effective debriefings achieved? What were the approaches and techniques that worked best? What were the approaches to be avoided? The debriefs revealed the fault lines, the reflexive words or actions that doctors and other clinicians defaulted to in stressful situations. "The faculty members are not pointing out what an idiot you are, but actually formulating questions and facilitating the discussion, because you want the participants to self-discover," says Gallo. "During the debrief you ask questions such as, 'what went well for you? How did the whole thing feel?' And people pick up where they could improve. Video and audio recordings of the sessions help make for a richer post-simulation debriefing." In debriefing sessions doctors, nurses and others saw what they were doing was ineffectual or not quite right or even counterproductive. Gallo has long since lost count of the number of *aha!* moments for doctors, nurses, other clinicians, and administrators in the sim center.

"No matter how experienced we are, we always need practice," she says. "Research indicates that the way you create mastery is through deliberate practice. Look at professional athletes who practice much more than they play in games. The same with concert pianists, chess players, people at the top of their game. You have to deliberately practice what you want to master and you need continuous immediate feedback so you don't develop your own belief system that what you are doing is right."

"It's one thing to read about it and quite another to actually experience it."

Dr. Barry Kanzer from the Department of Radiology at Long Island Jewish Medical Center works with the CLI team to teach residents and nurses safe ways to deal with patients who experience an allergic reaction to contrast material (commonly called contrast "dye") in imaging tests. Severe allergic reactions are rare but can occur without warning. Kanzer and his colleague Dr. Lawrence Davis, Vice Chair of the Department of Radiology, realized several years ago that because allergic reactions are infrequent, nurses and physicians had limited clinical experience dealing with them. There are cases when a patient can develop life threatening difficulty in breathing immediately after IV contrast is injected. Dr. Kanzer, who also serves as Assistant Professor of Radiology at the Hofstra Northwell School of Medicine, found a number of years ago that doctors and nurses did not treat such cases in a consistent and effective manner. In fact, Kanzer found that there was no standard treatment in effect in such cases and he set out to work with the CLI team to create a standard approach, through the use of simulation. The goal was to set a standardized approach for clinicians to confidently recognize and treat contrast reactions with the ultimate goal of improved patient safety.

In a typical session, Dr. Kanzer gathers at the PSI with a group of six radiology residents and five nurses. He explains that their session will consist of five different scenarios in which a simulated patient would present with a variety of adverse conditions following intravenous contrast administration. The nurse and/or resident will be called to see a mannequin or standardized patient in a room simulating a CT scanner. A hospital stretcher simulates the CT bed and the room has vital sign monitors, oxygen, various medications, and a phone to call for help to add to the realism. The hi-fidelity mannequin has pulses, heart and lung sounds, variable pupil size, can open and close its eyes, and can have tongue swelling. The PSI staff can also speak for the mannequin. A CT technologist is also present to alert the nurse or physician for the need for help and to provide assistance. The participants are oriented to the medications that are at their disposal prior to the scenarios. Watching through a one-way mirror, CLI staff members control the scenario with computers and provide verbal cues. Kanzer also sits in the control room directing the scenario and observing the participant's performance while other participants watch the scenario remotely so that they can gain from the experience as well. In one of the scenarios the CT technologist calls a nurse to see a patient who has a scratchy throat and is having trouble breathing after a contrast injection. Kanzer has the CLI staff provide a rapid heart rate, low blood pressure and a high rate of breathing. The patient's appearance and vital signs indicate a moderate reaction that must be diagnosed and treated immediately. What should the nurse do? She listens to the patient's heart and lungs, obtains vital signs and recognizes that an allergic reaction has occurred. She calls a Radiology resident to the room and together they decide on a course of action: fluids, oxygen, and an injection of epinephrine. They also call for EMS to send an ambulance. Watching from the control room, Kanzer instructs the CLI staff to have the patient's condition slightly worsen, despite the initial treatment undertaken. The nurse and resident reassess the situation and decide to administer another dose of epinephrine. At this point the patient starts to improve. Kanzer enters the simulation room acting as an EMT to take a report from the nurse and resident and the scenario is ended.

Everyone knows, of course, that this is not a real patient in crisis, but the simulation is so authentic in so many ways—every patient has an ID band with a name, date of birth, and allergy information and other identifying characteristics—that it *feels* real. "The simulation sessions are a way to make it more real," says Kanzer. "There is no substitute for being put on the spot. It's one thing to read about it but quite another to actually experience it." As Kanzer expects, the nurses and residents generally react very well to each scenario. They are caring, well trained professionals, but are not perfect. In another scenario a nurse enters the room to find the patient completely unresponsive. In the stress of the moment she neglects to obtain vital signs in order to adequately assess the patient and elects to immediately call for a physician. In another scenario, a resident enters the room and correctly starts appropriate treatment including giving an epinephrine injection, but neglects to don gloves which protect both the patient and resident.

Kanzer, CLI staff, and participating residents and nurses conduct a debrief after the scenario which provides an opportunity to ask some questions and engage in discussions with the goal of addressing gaps in knowledge and performance. "These scenarios, in a way, are just an excuse to do the debrief," he says. "We have an open discussion about how the participants felt, what they felt was happening, how and why they provided the treatment they did, and what they could have improved upon. We also talk about communication skills, focusing on the report given to EMS at the end of the scenario." During the debrief session, Kanzer speaks in a calm, comforting voice complimenting team members for things they did—for their compassion, their diagnosis, etc. "You guys did a really good job evaluating the patients." He emphasizes that they assessed the five things that are valuable in evaluating a patient quickly: blood pressure, heart rate, the patient's voice and appearance, pulse strength, and breathing, whether it is rapid, shallow or slow. Then he begins a discussion asking one person: "I noticed that you didn't put gloves on when you entered the room." In the stress of the moment, the person forgot to do so. Kanzer reminds the team that putting gloves on in treating a patient must be second nature.

"How is fluid helping the patient?" he asks another team member, his way of saying you did the correct thing, do you understand why you did what you did? "You elevated the arm, why did you do that? I notice you didn't hook up the vital sign monitor. I wonder why you would do that? Anybody else, would you do vital signs on this patient?" And, of course, the answer is yes, definitely. Again, in the stress of the moment they forgot to hook up the monitor. A teachable moment!

"Barry Kanzer's group is focusing here on a high risk event that is quite rare," says Gallo. "These are the kinds of events that people are often not prepared for because they happen so infrequently, but when they do happen they can be very serious for the patient. So practicing them is the key to safety. It is very similar to aviation. There was a situation on

JetBlue a few years ago with a plane coming in for a landing in California and the front part of the landing gear, the front wheel, wouldn't come down straight. The pilot kept circling and trying different things but nothing worked. Meanwhile, the whole thing is being broadcast live on CNN—the whole world is watching including the passengers on the plane! Finally, he gets the plane down and when they interview him they say, 'how did you ever land the plane with the wheel like that?' and he said, 'we practice this in simulation all the time.'"

"What we've got here is failure to communicate."

Comparing health care to aeronautics is helpful and instructive in many ways, but it only takes us so far. In reality, the challenges faced by clinical teams in health care are often more complex than those faced by airplane crews. While the mechanics of flying an airplane are complicated, the realities of delivering care day-in and day-out in a pressurized clinical setting take a toll. Thus, the burnout we see in so much of the health care universe these days. Gallo and Dowling wanted CLI to provide highly reliable guidance to teams on work that is repetitive and, to a certain extent, mechanical, such as the treatment protocols for patients allergic to contrast dye, but they also sought to develop programs for more complex situations involving the kinds of human interactions that are part of the daily business of health care.

In 2016, Dr. Miriam A. Smith brought this sort of challenge to CLI. Dr. Smith is chair of medicine at Long Island Jewish Forest Hills Hospital where she also supervises the residency training program. At the same time, she oversees a large number of other doctors in private practice who serve as attending physicians at the hospital. In 2015, she came to believe that the great majority of attending physicians, while very good doctors, were doing a poor job of teaching residents. The attendings are busy men and women who would often move swiftly through their work with patients while paying little attention to using patient care as an opportunity to teach residents.

Her observation was confirmed when she saw poor patient satisfaction scores of attendings and below average ratings by residents of the attending physicians. Smith spent some time talking privately with attendings and residents. It became quite clear that there was a communications gap between the two and that the residents, in particular, felt that the educational aspect of their training—learning from attendings—was suffering. Several attendings also voiced concern that residents were not consistently communicating patient issues with them.

Smith is not unsympathetic to the attendings. She understands that they are extremely busy and under pressure to produce; that their compensation in many cases has been reduced over time; and that they must achieve a certain volume to make ends meet. As a physician who also possesses an MBA, Smith gets the financial side of the business, but she also believes that there is an obligation to take the time needed to teach residents. "We run a robust resident training program and all the attendings know that," she says. "Residents are taking care of attendings' patients in the hospital and I would ask attendings if they remember when they were residents. The expectation is that you give them a little time." It was not that all of the attendings ignored the younger doctors. In fact, Smith had a number of doctors who were also extremely busy and under pressure who would nonetheless happily spend time with residents, acknowledging and appreciating the work they did caring for patients.

Smith went to CLI for help. The CLI team conducted a series of focus group interviews—two sessions with attending physicians and two sessions with residents. In all, about 30 attendings participated in the focus group sessions while about 30 residents attended those sessions. What emerged from these group interviews, guided by CLI staff, was consistent with what Dr. Smith had observed. The view of residents was that the attendings were supposed to help educate them; that the environment was supposed to be one of learning, yet from the residents' perspectives little instruction was happening.

Says Smith: "Residents felt that the attendings would say, 'this is my patient. Get an x-ray and give her five days of antibiotics,' versus saying, 'I am concerned about pneumonia in this patient. She is not improving. This is the symptom. What would you suggest as a possible treatment?' They were telling them as opposed to including them."

The CLI team offered some feedback to Smith and she wrote a series of brief cases drawn from real-world experience. Prior to the simulation sessions, CLI staff members trained standardized patients—actors skilled in playing the roles of patients and family members. The team also coached fourth year medical students who participated in the simulated events as standardized interns. The simulation sessions were mandatory for the Long Island Jewish Forest Hills attending physicians, who were told at the start to interact with patients and residents as they usually did. Between cases, the CLI personnel conducted a debrief with the physician participants on how to improve for the next case. Each simulated interaction at the patient bedside ran for about ten minutes. The debrief sessions in between, where each participant offered feedback, were about 20 minutes. The teams went back in for an additional simulated session, then gathered for a final, 30 minute debrief.

Just as with the case of Dr. Kanzer and his team, the power of simulation is its ability to replicate reality. Narrowing the power gradient in medicine has never been easy. Attendings have always held power over residents and other trainees but the lessons of Crew Resource Management make clear that for the safety and well-being of patients (and staff), that power gradient is dangerous. The attendings received feedback from the standardized patient and resident on the way they communicated. The reviews were not all glowing. In subsequent simulation sessions many, though not all, improved. Because this is a stubborn problem—and some attendings are resistant to change—the residents now provide ratings of the attendings on a variety of communications matters every six months. "We focused on the interactions between attendings and residents and it was clear that the attendings came away with a greater awareness of what they should be doing with residents at the bedside," says Smith. The anecdotal response from attendings was generally quite positive. The real test came with measurable feedback months later when Smith assessed the interventions. She found that when attendings were coached between the two simulated sessions, they clearly improved in the second case. She also found an overall improvement in patient satisfaction scores at Forest Hills. The people she considered higher performers scored very well on the simulation, but she was disappointed that more attendings did not score well. "If you look at the individual attending scores, it looks like some people did not really engage in the exercise," she says. "The high performers did well while those in the middle of the pack have some room to grow and this was probably a benefit for them." Overall, the initiative required a good deal of time, planning and execution, and, she concluded, "was probably a worthwhile endeavor."

"How can you be a great organization without lifelong learning?"

In the dozen years since the founding of CLI, the simulation center has grown from a 5000 square foot facility with a single simulator to a 40,000 square foot complex with 20 high fidelity simulators. Through the years hundreds of teams have built simulation scenarios that can be used over and over again; simulation programs for cardiothoracic surgeons and their teams, for emergency medicine, perinatal medicine, perioperative services, and on and on. CLI has grown through the years to the point where it is now part of the DNA of the Northwell organization. "If you said that we are going to shut down CLI and the Patient Safety Institute there would be organizational pushback," says Gallo. Many thousands of Northwell staff members—doctors, nurses, pharmacists, medical assistants,

administrators—have come through CLI for at least one program and over time it has become the go-to place for people
throughout the organization who want to improve many
aspects of care for patients.

While the competition in health care for patients is fierce,
so, too, is competition for employees and CLI has played a
role in the education and training of employees at all levels of
the organization. Part of the personnel strategy at Northwell is
to train people already in existing roles, particularly men and
women in leadership positions. Another aspect to personnel
development is to make sure that talented people are brought
to the fore and highlighted by their bosses. Dowling has made
clear that talented people belong to the organization—not
to a particular department or job. "The talent belongs to the
organization and the CEO will distribute that talent where he
believes it is needed to go," says Gallo. "If you have a really
top-notch person at North Shore University Hospital and they
are needed in Syosset, they go to Syosset." This was a challenging cultural change initially. Some bosses didn't like it
because it meant they would lose their best people—people
they had trained and developed. Some people didn't like having to move from one part of the organization to another. But
after a couple of years there was a general acceptance that
this was the new way of doing business at Northwell. The
model here, says Gallo, was large corporations where gifted
leaders are moved to various aspects of the company to learn
and develop and "not to just go into finance and you die in
finance."

"Mike wanted a different pathway to the leadership pipeline," says Gallo. "Around 2004 we talked about it internally
and we created an administrative fellows program with the
idea being that every year we would try and attract some
of the very best people from around the country." Gallo
was leading HR at the time and she put out word through
the American College of Health Care Executives looking

for young people who were in the process of completing graduate school in a variety of disciplines from economics to business to health policy. From the start, there were more than one hundred applicants for five fellowships. After a rigorous selection process, the five fellows arrived at Northwell for a one year fellowship in which they worked their way through four different rotations including working in a tertiary hospital, a community hospital, corporate headquarters, and then an additional area which could be the emergency services line, the insurance company or any number of other possibilities. Through the years these fellows have proven be among the best leaders in the organization. Talent is also developed from within via a program aimed at identifying employees with high potential for leadership.

"When we see a gap where we think we need to get leadership to we go to CLI," says Joe Moscola, Human Resources chief. "There's a jump, for example, between the front line manager and the middle manager and it is fairly large. How do you get someone from here to there in a seamless, more effective way? One part is how to improve their communications skills and another is understanding and improving their emotional intelligence. If you are aspiring to be a nurse manager you have to focus on quality while you focus on budget and manage the schedule. You need to understand how to lead teams." Moscola represents Dowling's somewhat idiosyncratic approach to personnel management. In many cases through the years, Dowling has appointed people to positions in areas where they possessed no previous professional experience. Gallo, for example, had no experience starting and running a corporate university. Moscola had no experience in HR prior to Dowling appointing him to lead HR in an organization with more than 60,000 employees. Dowling likes to bring in people who have clean slates and open minds and carry none of the standard or traditional approaches to a particular role.

Health care is a learning industry, but not every health care organization is a learning organization. Many hospitals and physician groups and integrated systems, in fact, are not learning organizations. That is to say they do not put a priority on continuous learning throughout the career of a doctor, nurse, or administrator. Perhaps it is considered too time consuming or too expensive—even unnecessary. After all, the men and women who walk into hospitals and clinics each day are some of the most highly educated people in the world. An emphasis on learning means that people's minds have to be open. It helps keep people humble. It reminds them regularly that they need to listen and absorb lessons and perspectives from others; that they have to test their own, long-held, assumptions.

"How can you be a great organization without investing in people and lifelong learning?" asks Jeff Kraut. "How do you get people to think differently about problems and create a culture of innovation where there is no penalty for trying something and failing intelligently because that is part of the learning process. We learn from trying, not from being timid, and when we try sometimes we fail, but, in doing so, we learn."

Not all of the learning is done by internal Northwell people. Every year CLI hosts a group of military personnel from 106th Rescue Wing of the New York Air National Guard based out of Hampton Beach, New York. This team "deploys worldwide to provide combat search and rescue coverage for U.S. and allied forces." The CLI team runs the military people through a critical series of training sessions on bio skills. "They are amazing," says Gallo. "They are para-jumpers, medical special ops teams who parachute in to quickly care for injured soldiers and we put them through some great simulation training that I think they find really valuable in preparing for the important work they do."

In the 16 years since Michael Dowling's flight to Seattle, the Center for Learning and Innovation at Northwell has grown into the leading corporate learning center within health care. Gallo is recognized as one of the nation's leading experts[5] in corporate education within health care as well as in simulation-based training. Dowling and Gallo talk often about the future of CLI and how it will need to adapt to stay current. "Given everything we have done we have to keep asking ourselves the question, where do we go next?" says Dowling. "CLI has grown tremendously with programs in many different areas.[6] Given the millennial nature of the population, given the clinical aspects of the way healthcare is going, given the digital world we are getting into, given the way now people in the future are going to learn—differently even than 10 years ago—what do we do now for the next 10 years? What is CLI 2.0? For example, what about having much more e-learning programs and virtual reality? What about having programs that center around consumerism? Whole cadre of programs dedicated to the concept of consumerism? How do we educate for what is regarded as population health? Nobody has defined population health, everybody talks about. It is apple pie and motherhood but what is it? If you were to develop a program for population health what would it be? Let's create it."

Health care leaders from throughout the country and the world—from China, Japan, Denmark, Australia, Saudi Arabia, and more—have visited CLI seeking to learn. For Northwell, CLI is an expensive venture and there is the possibility that, through teaching others, it could generate revenue, which Dowling says he would welcome, but he would never make a decision on CLI's future based on whether it was generating revenue. In an ideal world there would be sufficient revenue to make CLI self-supporting, but Dowling is quick to note that "I never use the word cost when it comes to CLI. I look at it as a human capital investment strategy."

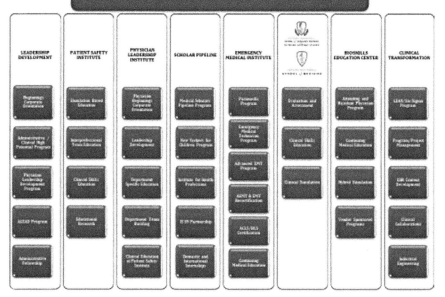

Endnotes

1. https://www.isixsigma.com/new-to-six-sigma/getting-started/what-six-sigma/.
2. http://www.academia.edu/8202128/crew-resource-management-in-healthcare.
3. http://www.ahrq.gov/teamstepps/instructor/essentials/implguide.html.
4. http://www.ahrq.gov/professionals/education/curriculum-tools/teamstepps/simulation/index.html.
5. Along with her colleague Dr. Lawrence Smith, Gallo edited the book Building a Culture of Patient Safety through Simulation: An Inter-professional Model.
6. Chart representing evolution of Center for Learning and Innovation.

Chapter 4

Redefining Medical Education: Creating the Hofstra Northwell School of Medicine

"The forces of change are again challenging medical education, and new calls for reform are emerging."

Carnegie Foundation

From Abraham Flexner to Michael Dowling

Michael Dowling was mystified by the way doctors were educated and trained. Why, he wondered, were they so out of sync with the reality of modern health care? "If you want to change the way medicine is delivered—and you have to do that—then you have got to train people differently," he explains. "Medical education I have always felt was just not done right. I was always fascinated with the fact that they would have a student in a school in the classroom for years and then put them into a big hospital. This is not where the bulk of the care is going to be delivered in the future so you are not training these students for the future that is going to exist, you are training them for the realities of the past. If the future of most health care delivery will not be in a hospital then why are you putting them in a hospital?"

If Dowling had ever doubted the need for a new type of medical education, he was persuaded one day during an orientation session with a group of students and residents. "I remember talking to them about quality metrics that as a health system we have to get right, but it was clear they didn't understand what I was talking about. I'm looking around the room and nobody is getting it and I think, 'well, maybe they can't understand me because of my Irish accent,' but that wasn't the issue. It turns out they had no clue about quality metrics. The whole system is moving toward more focus on quality metrics—sepsis, medication errors, infections, overall mortality—everything. I said, 'you learned about this in med school?' They said, *no*. 'Did your school ever tell you about quality outcome metrics?' *No*. 'What about community-based care?' *No*. 'What about the integration of behavioral health with primary care?' *No*. I thought, what are they teaching them? *What in hell is going on here?*"

Abraham Flexner wondered the same thing, although he was thinking about it a hundred years before Michael Dowling. Flexner was a researcher at the Carnegie Foundation for the Advancement of Teaching and he would prove to be one of the most influential people in the history of modern medicine. Some time during 1908, Flexner set out to visit every existing medical school in North America and to determine the level of quality in each facility. Visits to 155 medical schools later, Flexner had his answer: The overall quality of medical education was abysmal—so bad that it was dangerous. He issued a public warning to all Americans and Canadians to beware; to recognize that the doctors they were going to for care had nearly all been through educational programs of little or no value. Flexner found that most medical schools were profit-driven and ignorant of science; that these schools provided students with questionable curricula, substandard facilities, and very little science-based learning.

Looking back from 2016, it seems unfathomable to think that the great medical schools of the United States were anything less than exemplary. Throughout most of the twentieth century, American medical schools have been among the most elite educational institutions in the world, teaching millions of excellent doctors their craft and science while achieving some of the most important medical breakthroughs in history. These are homes to Nobel laureates where our very brightest young men and women learned to perform miracles! And for that, society owes a great debt to the work of Abraham Flexner. The Carnegie Foundation reports that "within a decade following Flexner's report … a strong scientifically oriented and rigorous form of medical education became well established."

More than a century after Flexner, however, there is once again a need for change within medical education. The Carnegie Foundation, diligent in their 109 years of research on this topic, has found that while transformative improvements came in the wake of Flexner, the "structures and processes" of medical education "have changed relatively little since" that time, and that "the forces of change are again challenging medical education, and new calls for reform are emerging." Carnegie notes that although "medicine and the sciences underpinning it have made … transformative advances since Flexner's report … *once again, our approach to education is inadequate to meet the needs of medicine.* Ossified curricular structures, a persistent focus on the factual minutiae of today's knowledge base, distracted and overcommitted teaching faculty, archaic assessment practices, and regulatory constraints abound."[1]

"Let's build a medical school."

It was clear by the start of the twenty-first century that the United States suffered from a shortage of physicians and the outlook suggested that in the coming years there was a possibility that the shortage could evolve into a full-blown crisis. This doctor shortage was not easily solved. The number of seats in American medical schools was rigidly fixed and strict regulations govern who may open a new medical school in the United States and under what circumstances. One result was that many of the newly minted doctors practicing each year had been educated in other nations. Did it make sense that a third or more of new doctors each year in the U.S. were coming from overseas? Even at a time when tens of thousands of highly qualified, passionate young students in America were unable to get into a U.S. medical school? From about 1970 to the turn of the century barely a handful of new medical schools opened, even as the population was growing older and an epidemic of chronic conditions washed across the land. A consensus emerged soon after 2000 among regulators and policy makers calling for existing medical schools to admit a few more students and for some universities to build new medical schools. Adding more students to a medical school class was doable at most institutions, but opening a new medical school is an enormous undertaking that very few institutions are equipped to handle. For some years, Dowling had been opposed to starting a new medical school. He made his opposition quite clear internally with other senior leaders and members of the board. For one thing, he was concerned about the enormous expense of a medical school. For another, he did not believe that Northwell had the people on board needed to get such a school up and running. It was ironic that Northwell was already deeply into the work of training physicians: About 800 residents from several different medical schools were rotating through various Northwell hospitals. And he also knew that without a medical school, Northwell would not achieve the truly elite status among major provider groups to which it aspired. The idea of starting a medical school kept coming up at regular intervals. What could be more consistent with Dowling's almost religious belief in the power of education than to teach a new crop of young physicians? What, exactly, might such a school look like? Dowling wasn't yet sure, but he knew he wanted something radically different than the existing medical school model and he also knew he needed experienced—and highly creative—physicians to lead the way. In 2006, he found them.

Drs. Lawrence Smith and David Battinelli knew medicine and they knew medical education. In a way, these two men had been preparing throughout their professional lives to disrupt medical education at a fundamental level. Smith trained at the University of Rochester in the 1970s when it was in the vanguard of new thinking about medical education. He subsequently practiced internal medicine in the U.S. Army during the waning days of the Vietnam War. Later, he went on to work as a primary care physician on Long Island and to lead the teaching programs at Mount Sinai School of Medicine and eventually rose to the position of Senior Associate Dean for education. Dowling was drawn to Smith's creativity and recruited him to Northwell in 2006 for the position of chief academic officer and then chief medical officer for the Northwell system. Smith and Battinelli had worked closely together in various educational venues and, in 2007, Smith recruited Battinelli to the position of chief academic officer at Northwell. Battinelli, a native New Yorker, (he was born at Mount Sinai Hospital), spent a good deal of his early career in Boston integrating training programs at three large academic medical centers. His interest in medical education grew as he ran an educational training program for students and residents at Boston City Hospital, Boston University Medical Center, and the Jamaica Plain Veterans Administration Medical Center, all academic affiliates of Boston University School of Medicine.

Through the years Dowling had engaged in casual discussions with Stuart Rabinowitz, President of Hofstra University, a private institution located in Hempstead, Long Island, just a few miles from the Northwell headquarters, about the possibility of joining forces. Northwell and Hofstra had collaborated on a couple of educational programs but discussions about a medical school never went anywhere until 2008. During a breakfast meeting one morning, Dowling and Rabinowitz agreed that it would make a lot of sense to create a partnership and start a medical school and with Smith and Battinelli in his lineup, Dowling was ready to go. "Stu and I discussed it and agreed that maybe we should think about doing something," says Dowling. "A week later we had another breakfast, this time Larry and I met with Stu Rabinowitz, and by the end of the breakfast we said okay, 'let's build a medical school'."

Stu Rabinowitz and Hofstra were solid partners in the venture. Rabinowitz was an accomplished attorney who had served as dean of the Hofstra School of Law for a dozen years before becoming president of the university in 2000. In some respects Dowling and Rabinowitz were cut from a similar cloth of public-spiritedness. For many years Rabinowitz had served on multiple public boards and committees. He also shared Dowling's vision for medical school graduates who, as Rabinowitz put it, would go out into the world "not just as doctors, but as innovators and leaders who will transform their profession for decades to come." He saw the new medical school as attracting "new research and cutting-edge scholarship" to Hofstra while providing the New York "region with better health care resources" and increasing the university's standing internationally.

While Dowling wasn't at all sure what the school would be like when it was up and running, he was certain that he wanted it rooted in the future—in the way medicine will be delivered in the years ahead. He had confidence that Smith and Battinelli were the right doctors to bring the school to life. In existing medical schools, the pattern through the years showed that making any kind of substantive curriculum changes—often in the face of opposition from faculty in siloed departments—was nearly impossible. Northwell, however, was free of the baggage existing academic departments typically carried. In one sense, Northwell had a clean slate. It also had a number of assets including the Northwell corporate university, called the Center for Learning and Innovation, more than a dozen hospitals, several thousand physicians as potential faculty members, millions of patient visits each year, a large and growing research facility, a fleet of more than 100 ambulances, and many years of teaching the third and fourth years for other medical schools.

In 2008, the Northwell trustees and the Hofstra trustees approved the medical school urging newly-appointed Dean Larry Smith to propel the school into the ranks of the top ten rated medical schools in the country. "I said, 'well, we will do our best,'" Smith recalls. "It will only take about 150 years to get into that group."

Audacious Ambition

In fact, the ambition for the medical school from the start was far greater than to become one of the top schools in the country within a decade—it was to do nothing less than *revolutionize medical education*. "We set out to redefine medical education," says Smith. "By 2005, everybody was dissatisfied with the traditional curriculum. We made a conscious decision that we were going to get on a national map because we were going to radically create an upheaval in how you trained doctors." This upheaval would be manifest in the mission and curriculum. "We wanted to use one of our strengths—the huge expanse of this health system—to focus on outcomes and population health," says Smith. This was new. Traditional medical schools focused on treatment of particular diseases in individual patients along with scientific research. "We do forty or fifty million dollars-worth of NIH research," Smith says. "Places such as Columbia and Harvard, in contrast, were so far ahead in this race that we are never catching them. But in population health we touch four million people a year. There are very few organizations doing that. Our research focus was going to be population health." This approach goes to the heart of what has become true north in health care—the Triple Aim, a term which describes a simultaneous aspiration for excellent patient experience of care (including, quality, access, safety), along with excellent population health management, while also lowering costs. Virtually every major provider organization in the United States is in pursuit of the Triple Aim and Hofstra Northwell School of Medicine's approach aligns the school with the central overall aspiration in health care today.

From the start, scores of Northwell physicians weighed in with suggestions on what would make a new medical curriculum great. "We had people come out of the woodwork to tell us everything that we should be doing," Battinelli recalls. "It became a sort of standing joke. Everyone—no matter whether it was 1970 when they graduated, or 1980, or 1990, or 2000—these were all physicians who by definition decided they had turned out perfect so we should do exactly what they did." But Smith and Battinelli wanted to pull back from the crowd. It was not that they did not welcome ideas and suggestions from others—quite the contrary. But they wanted the process of creating the new school to embrace the idea of radical change typically shunned in medical education. Why radical? Because the current model was outdated with "ossified curricular structures," in the words of the Carnegie Foundation report indicating not merely that medical education had not changed sufficiently, but that it had *lost its capacity to change*; that it was fossil-like.

Smith and Battinelli knew this. They had seen and felt this ossification for years and they sought to develop the new school based on exhaustive research into what new innovations were working in medical education and what traditional approaches should be avoided at all cost. They wanted to find the great ideas out there around the country, around the world. Not just in medical school but in other professional schools, as well. They were connected to a cadre of men and women throughout the country whose mission was to change the way doctors are educated. Smith, who is 66 years old and white-haired, has the appearance of an old-time country doctor, yet possesses a palpable intensity as he thinks, talks, and moves with speed. Battinelli, 59 years old, has the look of a leading man and speaks carefully, with an air of reflection. The two physicians share a sense of urgency, a sense that they are eager to detonate the charges, blow up what exists, and start something thrilling and new. They share a sense of excitement that they have discovered, perhaps invented something new—something *better*. They wanted a new approach to medical education that would "still be viewed as creative, innovative, and nimble enough to continue to transform itself for the year 2020," says Battinelli. "We picked 2020 because our first class would not complete all of their medical training and be an independent practice until the year 2020."

They wanted to construct a foundational core of principles upon which the new school would be built, core values against which any decision could be measured. Says Battinelli: "The idea was that any time we would deviate from the core values this would be the Bible that pulls us back and says, 'no that is not right.'" The guiding principles are, for the most part, what would be expected from a new medical school, with a few exceptions—that the curriculum would be "built upon experiential and active small group case-based learning;" that there would be "*early meaningful* patient interactions"; and that the school would be focused on "learning rather than teaching," an enticing yet, initially perplexing idea. The guiding principles are intentionally "edgy," he says, "so they do not sound like somebody else's values. In some of our values we are using words like *intolerant*. Other people said, 'you cannot use the word intolerant in a value statement,' and we said that we were intolerant of those who accept the status quo.

The guiding principles were how we would implement the values, and they were very, very important." The difference between this approach and the traditional approach to medical education was most evident in the focus on experiential and small group learning; in "not memorizing facts;" in "early and meaningful patient interactions."

Like just about everything else at Northwell, the medical school aligns with a certain set of values and can be seen in the school's commitment to "establish a culture of community that will have a transformative role in the health of the public. We are committed to educating future physicians to embrace responsibility for the health of their communities, and to be activists who advocate at the local, regional, and national level for the best care for patients and their community. Fulfilling this value will be an important metric by which we will demonstrate our success as an institution."

Learning from Other Medical Schools

In 2009, Smith, Battinelli and a small cadre of medical school faculty and administrators set out over a two year period to visit schools in the United States, Canada, and Europe in search of ideas they could use to build their medical school. This research and learning expedition, which took Smith, Battinelli, and several colleagues to more than 20-plus locations, spoke volumes about their thinking. The tour and the thousands of hours they spent searching out experts and innovations, the countless hours listening and watching, made clear that they were saying: *We make no pretension that we know the answers, but we will* find *the answers.* There is also, in this two year long search for ideas, an echo through the ages from no less a personage than Abraham Flexner. Smith and Battinelli embarked on their travels 100 years after Flexner, and while they had no intention of visiting *every* medical school in North America, as Flexner had done, they nonetheless took their cues from his relentless inquisitiveness. They carried with them his passionate search for excellence as well as his commitment to see up-close, first-hand what was actually going on out there. Smith and Battinelli read the literature, studied the books and papers, but, like Flexner, they needed to see things for themselves.

In their travels they found many like-minded colleagues frustrated by their inability through the years to break through the status quo and change curricula, but they also discovered a gold mine of ideas that had been tested in a variety of places. "Most of the ideas were things that they had experimented with and were able to carry out for short periods of time, six weeks, sometimes as much as a year," says Battinelli. "There were places trying to accomplish what we thought we wanted to accomplish but most were only able to attempt small pilot programs and people who had worked on these great innovations would say to us, 'you have to take our ideas and integrate them over the full four years to prove it works better than the status quo'."

They knew which research to plumb and which people to talk to and certain papers and books led them to more research while, invariably, certain academic experts led them to others—nearly all thoughtful and generous with their time and ideas. They learned a good deal from the writings of David M. Irby and Molly Cooke, faculty members at the University of California at San Francisco as well as from faculty members at Stanford (Kelley Skeff and Georgette Stratos), Case Western Reserve (Terry and Dan Walpaw), Harvard (David Hirsh), the University of Rochester, Tufts, McMaster University, The Uniformed Armed Services at Hebert University, University of New Mexico and many others. There was a spirit of collegiality and willingness to share great educational ideas. There were no blueprints at the start but during the journey of discovery Smith and Battinelli experienced, as Smith recalls, "a million *aha* moments."

"Trust your students."

One of those moments came one day in 2008 when Smith was in Hanover, New Hampshire, visiting his son who was then a student at the Tuck School of Business at Dartmouth. Smith sat in on a day's classes with his son and saw the teacher sit by barely uttering a word. A bit of guidance here, a question there, but nothing more. The amazing thing, Smith realized, was that *the students were teaching themselves*!

"After the class I said to the professor, 'what's the deal here?' And she said, 'trust your students.' I saw a school which totally trusted its students. There was no teaching simple content—no accounting 101. The students were learning through cases." That discovery at Tuck was "life-changing" for Smith. "I knew then that the students' learning would be our only measure of success. We would try to test whether the students could apply knowledge rather than recall facts. The greatest doctors I knew and worked with were not the doctors who memorized the best, even though that is much of what medical school tested. The greatest doctors I knew were the ones who could sort through a complex case and make sense of sloppy data that emanates from the patient, often in critical situations. The great doctors can be comfortable with uncertainty and apply their critical reasoning."

"When I was in medical school, the best students in the class were defined by only one attribute, memory," Smith continues. "If you could memorize millions of unrelated facts and spit them back on a test, you were considered the smartest kid in the room. I was studying one night and I was talking with my wife and I picked up the phone book—remember when we had phone books? I was sitting there and I opened the phone book and she says, 'what are you doing?' I said, 'I am really getting good at this. I am just going to memorize the whole phone book. I am getting really good at mindless memory.' In the age of the internet and smart phones you absolutely do not need memory. In fact, I would argue you should never *trust* memory except for the things you do all of the time. How do we teach the concepts of science that drive how the human body works? How do we teach science at the conceptual level and minimize the need to memorize minutiae, and at the same time give people robust enough concepts that if they wanted to do research in an area or look something up in an area, they can quickly teach themselves that minutiae because they understand the concepts."

"They were stagnating the creative process—breaking the rhythm of creativity."

Collaboration was important to Smith and Battinelli. They wanted ideas not just from people throughout the world but from people within their own organization. Toward that end, they assembled course design teams of 50 to 60 people—physicians, nurses, affiliated health professionals, and administrators. They filled conference rooms with smart, experienced people, and many of them made invaluable contributions to the process of building a new school. But there was a certain point where that was no longer true; where a line had been crossed and Smith and Battinelli were accelerating forward while some of the people in those rooms were trying to pull them back. These were people, recalls Smith, "who began every sentence with, 'well, *when I was in medical school …*' These were the naysayers and we couldn't tolerate them any more so we gently asked them all to leave." This was no simple matter. These were colleagues, friends—people with important roles within the Northwell organization—surgeons, leaders, department heads. But Smith and Battinelli knew it was time to move on. They were committed to certain principles and practical approaches and the time for further discussion was past. It was time to act. They went to the *when-I-was-in-medical-school-people* and said, "listen, this is not a good fit." Some, overburdened to begin with, were relieved. Some were stunned; some quite angry. "But we didn't have the time to negotiate these false barriers," says Smith. "They were stagnating the creative process—breaking the rhythm of creativity."

As these groups worked toward creating curricula for the new school, Smith noticed an interesting trend. Based on his experiences in scores of meetings it was clear that "the most creative people were at the extremes of their careers and the least creative in the middle." He is not certain why this was the case but he says it could not have been more apparent. He speculates that people near the end of their careers feel a sense of freedom to say exactly what is on their minds, while the younger people had just been through the education and training process and "were willing to say what a lot of crap it was." The men and women in the middle were different, he says. "Most often they thought they had it all figured out."

"You are right there with patients who are sick or injured and scared."

But the reality was that nobody had it figured out. That, at least, was the lesson of what Smith and Battinelli had learned during their travels. Throughout their planning sessions and philosophical discussions, Smith, Battinelli and other members of the original core team kept returning to the idea that students learned best from patients and that students should be participants in the learning process rather than observers. A fundamental flaw in medical education, they believed, was that students never had direct interaction—real-life, *meaningful* interaction—with a patient until the third year of medical school. Health care had changed radically over the years, yet the vast majority of medical schools continued to teach in a manner that was reminiscent of the approach decades earlier. Yes, science and technology had made enormous leaps forward, but had pedagogy? The status quo was old, creaky, and dangerously outdated. The new world of medicine was patient-centered, yet medical students never got near patients until year three. There was a general belief within the medical community that medical students assigned to a hospital ward would see patients with virtually every known disease. And to a significant extent that was true fifty years ago, but as Smith puts it—"that's baloney now. My guess is somewhere between 60 and 80 percent of diseases are never admitted into the hospital anymore. But at almost every medical school almost all of their clinical time is spent in the hospital."

Smith was convinced, based on his own experience as a physician and on experiences of many doctors he had encountered throughout his career, that "nobody remembers anything that is not related to patients. I could say to 50 doctors, 'tell me what you learned in the first two years of medical school,' and they would look at me and say, 'I don't remember a single day. I have no idea. I know I did really well on a test because I was a great crammer, but if I learned anything, I certainly do not remember it now.' Undoubtedly, you learn *something*, but they will tell you that 'I have *never forgotten* what I learned in the context of a real patient.' And not as an observer either. I mean directly involved with a patient. So if that is the case, then why not embed real patients from day one so that nobody ever asks the question, 'why am I learning this stuff?' which I must have asked 10,000 times in the first two years of medical school."

Smith and Battinelli wanted students with patients out in the community in real-life, stressful situations and that was great in theory, but you cannot send students out there with zero training. Smith had an idea. "What if we started them off from day one in accelerated Emergency Medical Technician training and sent them out with ambulance crews?" That would certainly get them out into communities engaging directly with patients and it could happen in a matter of weeks with accelerated training. And there would be plenty of opportunity for work since the Northwell system included a fleet of more than 100 ambulances. Thus came a major curricula breakthrough: Immersing students in accelerated EMT class during their first eight weeks and putting them on ambulances responding to every conceivable kind of emergency calls. This meant students were involved clinically from day one, encountering patients in deeply stressful life experiences from the start. This connected the students immediately to the profound humanity at the core of medicine.

The work Smith and Battinelli were doing in creating the new medical school caught the attention of the prestigious British Medical Journal,[2] where Smith was quoted as saying that

> One of our core principles is medical students should encounter patients with ever increasing real responsibility for the patients.
>
> Therefore you have to have some kind of a skill set or else at the beginning all you do is watch. And this EMT curriculum kind of jump-started a real skill set. The other piece is we felt that the students should be part of disaster response for this region. And so the last thing they do in the first course is disaster drills at the New York City fire department training centre.
>
> In Hurricane Sandy, right next door to us at Nassau Community College, there was a shelter for the medically ill. They put out a call for any EMTs to help staff the shelter and our whole class just literally walked across the swamp that was the flooded area and ran that shelter for almost two weeks because they all were licensed EMTs and totally capable of functioning independently that way.

In addition to EMT training and work, during the same eight week period, the students were taught to conduct a full physical of patients, head to toe, and to take a comprehensive medical history. This is something medical schools typically teach over a couple of years. Smith and Battinelli wanted to teach it early on and then coach students over time to strengthen their knowledge and ability. Josh Newman is a second year student at Hofstra Northwell, found rapid immersion EMT program both scary and exhilarating. "It was overwhelming in a way, those first weeks riding in the back of an ambulance with patients," he says. "You are right there with patients who are sick or injured and scared. One of my first patients was an older man with a history of heart disease and he was experiencing chest pain. When we arrived in the ambulance he was at home, sitting in his living room. We did an EKG and it showed an abnormal rhythm. The reality was he could have deteriorated at any moment. We had to keep him calm and comfortable and we made it to the hospital."

Smith has a particularly apt analogy that speaks volumes about the early focus on direct patient intervention at Hofstra Northwell. "Let's say you wanted to learn how to play baseball," he says, "and I said to you, 'okay, I can teach you to play baseball. I want you to come to my baseball camp and every morning we will study the physics of fastballs, sliders, and curveballs.' You would learn some interesting things about different pitches but you would absolutely *not* learn how to hit a baseball."

"Maybe the students are telling you lectures are not the way they learn medicine."

Smith and Battinelli thought that lectures in medical school were a truly terrible way for students to learn, yet the notion that the curriculum would not include lectures—or would not include them as an essential teaching element—seemed nothing less than bizarre to most physicians. Lectures were the core of medical schools throughout the world. How on earth could students be taught unless there was a "sage on the stage"—experts in particular medical areas imparting their knowledge? Smith and Battinelli, however, had done their homework and they had an entirely different take on lectures. They found, for example, in medical schools not requiring attendance at lectures, that a majority of students stayed away. On average, only about one third of students at these institutions regularly attended lectures, yet most of these medical schools were training men and women who went on to become great doctors. So what was going on? "These students become brilliant physicians," says Smith. "At one of the very top medical school less than 20 percent of the students are going to lectures yet they go on to become great doctors. Maybe the students are telling you lectures are not the way they learn medicine." These students who avoided lectures were not lounging at the beach, says Battinelli. They were finding information and insights on the internet. "With smart phones and computers people can look things up immediately and not have to go to lectures," he says. "If you want a lecture on cystic fibrosis from the expert at Stanford you can find it online in two seconds."

One-on-One with Physician Mentors

Abraham Flexner's report triggered a revolution in medical education and within a couple of decades the quality of medical schools had improved dramatically and that quality continued to improve throughout most of the twentieth century. And then things started to slip. Schools were teaching students how to work within hospital settings when the vast majority of doctors would administer care in ambulatory rather than in-patient settings. UCSF Drs. Irby, Cooke and colleagues wrote in the *New England Journal* that the purpose of medical education is to transmit the knowledge, impart the skills, and inculcate the values of the profession in an appropriately balanced and integrated manner. "In the apprenticeship model of medical training that prevailed into the mid-nineteenth century," they wrote, "student physicians encountered this knowledge and these skills and values as enacted by their teachers in the course of caring for patients. How are knowledge, skills, and professional values represented in contemporary medical education?"

It was a good question and one that spoke directly to what Smith and Battinelli wanted to do at the new medical school. The article continued, noting that "responsibility for the care of patients is a powerful stimulus for learning, and active

learning requires that clinical skills, both cognitive and proce-
dural, be attained through the supervised provision of patient
care."

> As Flexner recognized, medical novices require the
> opportunity to practice skills under the guidance of
> experienced teaching physicians until they attain a
> high level of proficiency. Increasing attention to the
> quality of care, patient safety, [patient throughput],
> and documentation of care enhances medical prac-
> tice but threatens to relegate trainees to the role of
> passive observer.

Besides the work as EMTs, how else could Smith and
Battinelli get students in close touch with patients starting
early in their medical education and continuing over time?
And not as observers but as participants and real-world learners? What if they paired every student with a set of practicing
physicians to work side-by-side with the doctors taking care
of patients? Thus, came another major innovation: Students
would work alongside practicing physicians after just a few
months in school. They called this the initial clinical experience (ICE) and it cast students in the first three months of
school into the deep end of the pool, albeit with one-on-
one medical lifeguard alongside. The ICE program provided
training that was not crammed into the third year of medical school, as was tradition, but spread out over the first two
years. This would require special faculty members. Hundreds
of doctors throughout the Northwell system were eager to
join the faculty, but many of them, recalling their own days in
medical school, envisioned the role as a didactic one—doctor
in front of a classroom imparting wisdom to students. Many
physicians came to Smith and Battinelli saying they wanted
to teach in the medical school, often saying they could give
a high quality lecture on a given issue. When Smith and
Battinelli would tell these men and women that there would

be no lectures, there was puzzlement. Battinelli would say to prospective faculty members: "I will tell you what, if you think you can help us to define what the learning objectives we are seeking to accomplish should be (*and we cannot and will not teach everything*), and if you can help us design a learning experience (*non-lecture based*) and then create an assessment to determine if the experience provided resulted in learning, and then after all that, you develop a feedback process to constantly refine and innovate that objective, perhaps then we may have a role for you. Anything short of that ..." At this point, many prospective faculty members started backing away. "Half of them just called us lunatics and walked away, and the other half were interested and said they had been waiting for this for a long time," says Battinelli. "We said, 'you have to be willing to take a student in your practice and help them learn how to care for patients.' We said to the Ob docs, 'you have to let them work with pregnant patients and teach them how to examine women and when the beeper goes off they will meet you in labor and delivery and they will deliver the baby with you'." Within the initial clinical experience program each student works one-on-one with a set of physicians in a continuity relationship, alternating between: internal medicine, ob/gyn, pediatrics, surgery, and psychiatry for a minimum of four to five hours a week for two years.

Smith and Battinelli chose the faculty members carefully for they wanted doctors who would embrace the opportunity to bring an eager young medical student into their practice and teach them one-on-one while practicing at the front lines. Most faculty members, it turned out, loved the experience and were generous with their time as they made an effort to get the students as close to the reality of medical practice as possible. And in the vast majority of cases this meant very close indeed—right there at the physician's side in clinic, in the hospital, and in the OR. The idea that students with minimal training would be permitted to scrub into surgery seemed ridiculous initially. But as Smith notes, "eventually you are going into the OR and in the third year of med school, after sitting in the classroom for two years, going into the OR with no preparation. You are in there with a crowd of people and you are lucky if you can get to the front row. We are taking people in their fourth month of med school and surgeons working with them one-on-one teach them to scrub, hold a retractor, cut things, sew things. The first couple of times you are going to do nothing but scrub. Put the gown on. Feel comfortable. Move around and take a look. Make sure you do not pass out when I cut the guy. One of our guiding principles is continuity. As a faculty member I do not want to see a new student and believe me the patient does not want to see a new person every single time he shows up either. Our students form bonds and relationships with the doctors they work with and with patients. They help deliver babies and you go round and you see our students and on their iPhones they have pictures of the babies."

The initial clinical experience is embodied in the collaborative nature of the relationship between Dr. Robert Scanlon and medical student Ben Smith, who arrived at Dr. Scanlon's Ob/Gyn practice on Long Island, after a grand total of about ten weeks of medical school. During Scanlon's time in medical school back in the 1970s, students did not engage with patients directly until third year, after two years studying biological sciences. Preparation for this moment had begun a couple of years earlier when Smith and Battinelli had invited Scanlon to become part of the faculty, emphasizing that it would be very different from anything he had experienced. And it was. Scanlon had agreed to bring a medical student into his practice on a regular basis and teach that student by having the student work with him side-by-side. Consider the possible disruption. Scanlon is a busy physician with a couple of thousand patients, a schedule that runs from early in the morning until early evening and an office staff of nurses, and other professionals working at an intense pace every day all day. It takes a particular type of culture to welcome in a first year medical student.

Before Ben even arrived in the office, Scanlon and his team explained to patients what would be happening and they found that the overwhelming majority of patients were comfortable with the idea. "Ben didn't just fall out of the sky," says Scanlon. "We were careful in preparing our patients and our staff also. And Ben had just been through EMT training and had taken care of people in emergency situations on the ambulance. Also, Ben had just completed six years of military service so he was quite mature." That first day Ben arrived in a starched white jacket, shirt and tie, ready to go. Ben was unusually mature for a first year student. He was a graduate of the United States Military Academy at West Point and had served as Captain of an infantry company in Iraq (two tours). "When I was applying to medical school one of the things that attracted me initially was getting more exposure to patient care earlier on," he says. "The main reason most people want to go to medical school is to treat patients and in those first two years if you are only in a classroom that's not what you really want to do."

Scanlon and Ben developed a smooth rapport. Prior to a patient visit Scanlon and Ben would go through the patient list for the day and Scanlon would provide Ben with a brief description of each patient. When a patient arrived for the appointment, Scanlon and Ben would go into the exam room together and Scanlon would explain that Ben was going to go over some things and that Scanlon would be back in a few minutes. Ben would then take a basic history. *What are the issues? What brought you in today,* etc. Ben would then huddle with Scanlon for a moment (outside the exam room), explain the situation, then the two men would return to sit down with the patient. "You could see over time Ben's level of expertise and comfort increase steadily," recalls Scanlon. "He became a much better interviewer, a much better listener.

Initially, he would always defer to me but as the months went by we would go back in the exam room and he would retell the story with the patient."

The basic skill set for an Ob/Gyn doc is largely mechanical, says Scanlon: Pap smears; detecting and listening to the baby's heartbeat. A lot of that is learned on mannequins. But it was direct engagement with patients in the exam room that most advanced Ben's learning. "He was blessed to have the nicest patients," says Scanlon, "who taught him how to feel fetal heartbeat. They would teach him and say, 'no, push hard and you can feel it.' They became the teachers and that is where we needed to trust this model to work. The naysayers said patients will be too uncomfortable and do not want to be experimented on but that wasn't true."

From September to the following April, throughout his first year in medical school, Ben spent one afternoon per month in Scanlon's office, where he became part of the clinical team. Staff members in the clinic had all learned through an apprenticeship model, to one extent or another, and they welcomed Ben and took responsibility for helping to teach him. Everybody on the staff had someone who had at some point taken the time to help them, mentor them, and staff members were committed to doing the same for Ben.

"By the end of our time together Ben could, with my supervision, do the whole exam, take history, find heartbeat, tell me the position the baby was in, get a thorough obstetrical history, and he was very good with evaluating acute visits." Not all physicians serving as preceptors have the time to allow the student to engage directly in care, as Scanlon did with Ben, but, as Ben puts it, "when its executed in the ideal way it's a great way to do your first two years. You learn a lot in class but sometimes that doesn't really hit you with the context of it all. Then you see a patient who has something you studied in class and you have a different level of understanding." Over time, Ben also became invested in the well-being of many patients. There was one woman, in particular, who had encountered substantial barriers to pregnancy and, at a certain point, required corrective surgery. Ben made a point of being present for Julie's appointments and when the time for surgery arrived, Scanlon recalls that the surgical team gathered around Julie in the OR just before administering anesthesia. "We were all masked and gowned for the surgery and just as we were about to have the timeout Julie said to me, 'Dr. Scanlon, is Ben here yet?' Standing next to me, Ben said, 'Julie, I am right here with you.'"

Assess Knowledge-in-Action, Not Memorization

The radical nature of the proposed curriculum left many quite reasonable people uncomfortable. Smith, Battinelli and their colleagues, after all, were tearing down a revered old model of teaching doctors and building an almost entirely new structure in its place. *No lectures!?* Crazy. *Students teaching one another?* Come on. But Smith and Battinelli were way past that sort of thinking. They saw things from an entirely different perspective. "People criticized us as too learner-centered. 'No one should trust the learners that much,' they were telling us. So we said, 'if we cannot trust the top one-tenth of one percent of students in the United States, who are we supposed to trust?'"

Smith and Battinelli hate multiple choice exams and the cramming that invariably precedes them. They wanted to test their students in more meaningful ways that would both teach and assess students' broader abilities—the abilities most consistent with being a good doctor. They wanted depth and understanding, not surface recall. They also wanted students to have "a consistent pace," says Battinelli. "College is cram and regurgitate, or, as I used to say cram, regurgitate, binge drink, regurgitate again. So that is college or pre-med, but that is not life. You would kill yourself doing that for the rest of your life. You will hate what you do. You will burn out. We made a decision early on that if you get into our medical school, you are smart enough to be a doctor and we wanted students competing against a standard of excellence, not against the person sitting next to you. Our model of assessment is about coaching to excellence not about memorization."

At Hofstra Northwell they test every twelve weeks. The assessment period lasts for a full week and involves oral exams, written essays, standardized patient exams, and videotaped simulations—all toward testing the ability of students to "*apply knowledge in action*" to a particular clinical challenge. It is difficult to overstate the importance of simulation in testing the abilities of the students while, simultaneously, providing them with highly realistic, intense clinical challenges. Northwell's internal corporate university—known as the Center for Learning and Innovation was essential to making the medical school a rigorous and fruitful educational experience. And simulation—as close to the intensity of real-world patient encounters as possible—played a crucial role in both teaching and assessment. Says Smith: "In testing, we do not ask them what enzyme controls gluconeogenesis in the liver. We never ask that. Who cares whether you know that at that moment in time? No doctor who practices can ever remember that anyway. We do not ask recall questions. We ask, 'given the scientific concepts and principles you just studied for twelve weeks, here is a problem you never saw before. But we are telling you that the science you learned is the solution to this patient's problem, and go solve it.' That is how we test the students."

Some of the testing is formative while some is summative. Formative assessment aims to test as a means of helping and guiding a student to learn while summative assessment helps determine a student's final level of proficiency in a particular area. Battinelli has a pronounced preference for formative testing believing that, over time, it strengthens students' knowledge and ability to apply what they know. There are, however, dissenters in that area. Some educators suggest that the formative testing "is not high stakes enough," says Battinelli, but he sees it differently.

"I give them feedback on the history or I give them feedback on the physical and on their clinical thinking," he says, "but I am not easy on them. Recently I gave a student a lot of feedback and he said, 'if this was the sum of the end of the year would I have passed?' and I said, 'absolutely not, you're maybe 40 percent of the way on your physical and 60 or 80 percent of the way on your history. This is what you have to work on.' But it is formative." In the *New England Journal* article "American Medical Education 100 Years After the Flexner Report," the authors note that

> it has long been observed that assessment drives learning. If we care whether medical students and residents become skillful practitioners and sensitive and compassionate healers, as well as knowledgeable technicians, our approaches to the evaluation of learners must reach beyond knowledge to rigorously assess procedural skills, judgment, and commitment to patients. Self-assessment, peer evaluations, portfolios of the learner's work, written assessments of clinical reasoning, standardized patient examinations, oral examinations, and sophisticated simulations are used increasingly to support the acquisition of appropriate professional values as well as knowledge, reasoning, and skills. Rigorous assessment has the potential to inspire learning, influence values, reinforce competence, and reassure the public.

Smith and Battinelli decided that for the first two years students would be graded pass/fail. "We are about creating life-long learners and that meant creating the best possible non-competing but rigorous learning environment," says Battinelli. "The joke in medical education has long been that the way to get ahead in pre-med was to run faster than the other guy or put lead weights on the other guy. It has been a horribly competitive environment. One 'C' in four years and that may have been the end of you. It was ridiculous. We tell the kids that the only thing you will compete against is a standard of excellence. You will never compete against the person next to you. Everybody here is supposed to succeed. We want you competing against the standard of excellence. We will coach you to excellence. Here are your strengths. Our assessment models access critical reasoning. No one gets all right or all wrong. You are coached to excellence."

One particular quirk about testing has been and continues to be quite controversial. "We do not score on a bell shaped curve," says Smith. "We score against what we think the standard is. It is tough for people to digest. We do not give scores back to students and it drives them out of their minds. They get *meets expectations* or *does not meet expectations*. Then a small group gets a tag that says *meets expectations with recommendations,* which means you are on the borderline. The *meets expectations* students never see a score so they really do not know if they got a 99 or a 79 because that is not real life. We are not getting scores all the time. We are not going to define them by score anymore; we are going to define them *by their ability to do what they are supposed to do*. In our grading we say to the student, 'here are the things you are doing really well, congratulations. Here are the things you are not doing so well. Let us have a plan to work on it.' Because nobody does everything perfectly. It is a coaching model of grading as opposed to a hurdle." This has been controversial at the school in light of the fact that every teacher and student in the school has been accustomed throughout his or her academic careers to getting specific scores on a regular basis. "Students get upset so the faculty gets upset and early on they said, 'we have to abandon this.' But we are not going to abandon it."

Case-Based Curriculum

Smith and Battinelli found what they thought was a better way of teaching during Larry Smith's *aha* moment at Dartmouth—small groups of students collaborating on case studies. This is the PEARLS program—*patient-centered explorations in active reasoning, learning, and synthesis*—a case method where students focus on a specific medical topic each week. The journalist from the British Medical Journal was clearly intrigued with the PEARLS method, writing that "the cases are constructed so that the students identify what it is they need to learn to understand the science behind each case. Everything that happens in the week uses those cases as anchors and the theme of each session in the week unravels directly from that case."

In PEARLS, students in small groups of eight or nine students, meet three mornings a week for two hour sessions. During the Monday meeting they are given two clinical cases, about four to five pages each. With the faculty member present as a guide, the students read aloud through the cases stopping after each paragraph to determine what aspects of the case in that paragraph require a deeper research dive by the students. Here they define the learning objectives, which require additional research and study by students on their own time. David Elkowitz, Associate Dean at the school, explains that during the Monday session "students go one-by-one through the paragraphs of the case and stop at the end of every paragraph to discuss and identify potential learning issues or objectives. One learning objective might be 'describe a normal coronary circulation of the heart,' for example." All nine students are responsible for understanding the basics of all aspects of the case. Smith, Battinelli, Elkowitz and their colleagues believe that a student's ability to teach the material is a powerful indication that the student has learned the material. "And there is no divide and conquer," says Elkowitz.

"Every student works up every learning objective and identi-fies their sources."

Everything in PEARLS is done in the context of a complete patient story. Students rely upon textbooks and multiple online scientific sources to research their learning objectives, but the information they gather and the studying they do in various sciences relates directly to a patient case. When the students reconvene Wednesday morning they go through the case in detail, solving for all the challenging scientific areas identified on Monday and, in the process, testing and challenging one another in respectful and collegial ways. Every student in the group is expected to find a way to study and understand all the learning objectives for a particular case—anywhere from 10 to 20 for each case—and to come to Wednesday class well-prepared. The definition of well-prepared in this student-led model is that the student must have a firm enough grasp on the material to be able to teach it to fellow students. Because all members of the group learn collaboratively, everyone is both teacher and student able to teach a challenging clini-cal/scientific concept. Because PEARLS simultaneously has students learning from and teaching one another, it is all but impossible for any student to hide. The PEARLS approach demands intense preparation from every student for every class and essentially eliminates students skipping classes. During one PEARLS session in spring, 2016, eight of the nine group members raced through a challenging case. One stu-dent, however, stuck out for an obvious lack of preparation. At the conclusion of each PEARLS class, students spend a moment offering an assessment of the quality of the class and of their role in it. During the self-assessment portion this par-ticular student was clearly embarrassed by his lack of prepa-ration and promised his fellow students that "it will never happen again." This sense of accountability pervades the pro-gram. PEARLS demands maturity and commitment from every member of the group. There is a level of transparency where

it is clear in every session how well prepared each student is
for class and in the overwhelming majority of cases students
arrive extremely well prepared. Otherwise, the approach
would collapse on itself. One of the challenges in PEARLS
cases, says second year student Josh Newman, is figuring
out what aspects of the case are most important to learn and
understand. "On Monday we identify what we don't know in
a case," he says. "Every case has a goal and we have to decide
as a group what in the case is relevant to that goal. We need
to ask the right questions and we rely on each other in doing
this. The team nature of learning is that we rely so much on
each other that there is respect for the process and everybody
comes prepared."

After researching and studying the basics from learning objectives, students convene in class to push toward
higher order questions that build upon the learning students
have done on their own. Throughout these sessions faculty
members say surprisingly little—at least it is a surprise to
those steeped in a traditional pedagogic method. Much of
the faculty's work is done prior to classes when they gather
together—physicians from multiple disciplines—and write the
case. During class, faculty members facilitate this probing of
expanded understanding asking students: What exactly is your
question? Could you elaborate further? How could we verify if
that is true? Can you sketch that for us? What factors make this
a difficult problem?

On the surface, the PEARLs sessions appear relaxed but
it soon becomes clear to an observer that there is a palpable
sense of tension in the room. "In academics you need tension
because without tension there is no growth," says Elkowitz.
"Tension lives all over PEARLs. There is tension in the students learning how to speak to each other. Tension is being
put on the spot to be honest in group self-assessment, trying
to actively figure out an answer to somebody's higher order
question. We facilitate tension with a smile and with a good
attitude, but the tension is always there. The students have to

learn how to challenge one another respectfully and to not take anything personally, to leave their baggage at the door."

"The basic science departmental structure was really a relic of the late 1800s."

Typically, medical schools throughout the United States are organized into departments, often a dozen or more. Much good work is done within these sections, certainly, but over the years it has become clear that departments often act like siloes with department heads and members jealously guarding departmental turf. Neither Smith nor Battinelli believed this made much sense if the goal was the best possible quality of education for students and they decided that Hofstra Northwell medical school would have two departments—science education for teaching and molecular medicine for researchers. "Once we were free of departments and the challenges they bring, we were free to say, 'okay, what would be the most logical sequence of learning how the human body works?' We built a curriculum unfettered by department ownership where there was a team of faculty running each course. We actually figured out a logical way to roll out the human body in health and disease as opposed to which department gets the first course, and which department gets the second course." Smith told the British Medical Journal that

> "It was very clear that the basic science departmental structure, was really a relic of the late 1800s.
>
> Departments were named and siloed by the very earliest phases of biomedical science—names like physiology and pharmacology and microbiology and anatomy. Each one of these departments are vestiges of another era of science because amazingly now everybody's science looks almost the same no matter what department they're in. But those departments hung on to their turf with ferocity. So we decided not to have departments. So we have a department of

teachers called the department of science education and a department of researchers called the department of molecular medicine. And that's it.

That allowed us to ask the question: if we never had departments, what is the right sequence of learning about the human body in health and disease, as opposed to giving biochemistry a course here and anatomy a course there? How would we actually teach this if we didn't have to worry about the turf of departments?"

Smith and Battinelli realized that when launching an enterprise this radical, they needed to pay close attention to detecting flaws and they needed to be able to fix those flaws quickly. From the start, they were committed to a rigorous curriculum and, initially, that meant making sure that students came to class well-prepared. Toward that end faculty members assigned readings for each night but after only a couple of months students rebelled. One student printed out the readings for a single night and it totaled 200 pages of complex material. The pushback came not from a few students but from just about all of them and if Smith and Battinelli were going to trust their students they had to listen, and they did. "We were having them do assignments that seemed wonderfully comprehensive but really turned out to be more make work than anything else," says Smith. "All the students can't be wrong."

The solution was to define the areas students needed to understand before coming to class and to leave it up to the students how they would gain that knowledge—via internet readings, YouTube demonstrations, whatever helped the student learn. And it worked. But it also created some conflict within the faculty. "There were people who had ownership of these approaches" and they had worked long and hard to come up with a particular pedagogical approach they believed would work. When the approach didn't work—the 200 pages of reading per night, for example, "people who had ownership mourned."

Not surprisingly, a fair number of the students come from families where one or both of their parents are physicians, and, from the start, a funny pattern involving these parents emerged. They would corner Smith or Battinelli and say, "listen, I was miserable in med school—I hated it and my classmates did too, but now my kid is happy in med school. What is going on here?" *There was suspicion about the program because the students were happy!* There were other, less charitable criticisms. A number of naysayers early on said the students would not do well on standardized tests required to obtain a medical license because of the assessment methodology. The school will be unable to attract quality students because there is no proof the students can get into good post-graduate programs. "They would say, 'your students are going to fail all of the licensing exams'," recalls Smith. "'They are never going to get a residency.' Because everyone was convinced the licensing exams were just fact recall. By us not emphasizing that, we were going to handicap our students. It turns out actually understanding the science really helps on taking the test because our students are doing much better than the national mean on the exam with no effort in the curriculum to teach to this test." In fact, students at the medical school are among the most competitive in the nation, with MCAT and GPA metrics in the upper half of regional New York Schools. Students are an extremely diverse group in terms in racial/ethnic backgrounds, undergraduate institutions and majors, as well as states of origin. Once matriculating, students perform exceptionally well in the curriculum, founded on principles of integration and adult-learning. On national metrics, such as the United States Medical Licensing Examinations, students perform well above the national mean and in the range of the most competitive schools regionally and nation-wide. More than 70 percent of students complete research projects while matriculated and participate in numerous clubs and community service activities. At the end of medical school, more than 96 percent report being satisfied with the quality of their educational experience, a metric that compares very favorably against the nation.

One of the most important developments in the wake of the creation of the medical school has been the building of a graduate school of nursing—nurse-led—with a similarly radical approach to curriculum and training. Its founding dean, Kathy Gallo, was trained as a nurse, holds a doctorate in nursing, and started the Center for Learning and Innovation from scratch. The school's first cohort of 30 students was working their way through their second year in the Hofstra Northwell School of Graduate Nursing and Physician Assistant Studies during the winter–spring of 2017. The school offers a Master of Science Program with a major in Nursing with the aim to "graduate nurse practitioners who will be prepared to provide quality, holistic, scientifically sound, and patient-centered care."

Hofstra Northwell School of Medicine has graduated two classes thus far, which means its most advanced students are just into their second year of training. The school, in other words, is in its infancy. But there are some important signs at this stage worth considering. The school has attracted students with multiple different options in terms of the medical schools to which they were admitted and a number of students chose Hofstra Northwell instead of some of the most prominent names in the country. Also, every member of the classes thus far has found a placement in a residency program and a number of those are among the most competitive such programs in the country including Duke, Yale New Haven, Kaiser Permanente, and Mount Sinai.

One of the most interesting developments is that scores of visitors interested in the Hofstra Northwell curriculum have come to visit. Some of the visitors are from existing medical schools while others are from organizations planning to start a new medical school including Kaiser Permanente which is modeling a good deal of its new school on approaches from Hofstra Northwell. After spending at day at the school, Bonnie Bonita Stanton, MD Founding Dean at Seton Hall–Hackensack School of Medicine, wrote to Smith and his team: "WOW! I was and remain overwhelmed by the quality and originality of your curriculum, the obvious excitement on the part of the faculty and students and the amazing support system offered through the Center for Learning and Education and Bioskills Center. Each time I would think that I had just seen the capstone element of the School of Medicine—you would produce yet another equally stunning aspect that worked synergistically with every other aspect!"

One cannot help but wonder what the great pioneer Abraham Flexner would think of the new approach. Perhaps the best judgment on that question comes from the organization that knew Flexner best—the Carnegie Foundation. In the *New England Journal* the authors of "American Medical Education 100 Years after the Flexner Report," suggest that "no one would cheer more loudly for a change in medical education than Abraham Flexner. He recognized that medical education had to reconfigure itself in response to changing scientific, social, and economic circumstances in order to flourish from one generation to the next. The flexibility and freedom to change—indeed, the mandate to do so—were part of Flexner's essential message. He would undoubtedly support the fundamental restructuring of medical education needed today. Indeed, we suspect he would find it long overdue."

Endnotes

1. Malcolm Cox, M.D., Editor, David M. Irby, Ph.D., Editor; "American Medical Education 100 Years after the Flexner Report"; Molly Cooke, M.D., David M. Irby, Ph.D., William

Sullivan, Ph.D., and Kenneth M. Ludmerer, M.D.; *New England Journal of Medicine*; Carnegie report, "American Medical Education 100 Years after the Flexner Report."

2. David M. Irby, Molly Cooke, Bridget C. O'Brien. Calls or reform of medical education by the Carnegie Foundation for the advancement of Teaching: 1910 and 2010. *Academic Medicine*, 2010 Feb;85(2):220–7.

Chapter 5

Emergency Preparedness

> *"Emergency management to me is very, very important as a central competency that you should have in any large health system, especially in New York. We started to develop our emergency management infrastructure before 9/11 on the basic assumption that bad things are going to happen and we have to be ready."*

Michael Dowling

"This is going to be the guy."

FBI Special Agent John O'Neill was frustrated. O'Neill was an expert in counter terrorism but he was having a hard time getting people to listen to him. He was sure something was looming, something very bad, and it was important that he get the attention of health care leaders in New York City. But people he spoke with, while respectful of his position, didn't ever seem to *do* anything as a result of what he told them. And then things changed. O'Neill got the ear of a Robert A. Rosen, Northwell Health trustee, and at Rosen's behest a meeting was scheduled in the Fall of 1998 between O'Neill and Kathy Gallo, chief of Northwell Emergency Services. Gallo drove to an FBI facility in upstate New York and watched a small outdoor ceremony for agents graduating from a training program. O'Neill addressed the graduates and their families, while Gallo watched from a picnic table nearby. O'Neill was something of a renegade. He had worked his way up through the FBI ranks to become chief of the bureau's counter terrorism section and he had a particular expertise in the bombing of the World Trade Center in 1993. O'Neill doggedly pursued Ramzi Yousef, the al Qaeda operative who was the leader of that attack, and in large part due to O'Neill's efforts, Yousef was captured in Pakistan and later tried and convicted of terrorism in the United States.

After the graduation ceremony, O'Neill introduced himself to Gallo and thanked her for taking the time to meet with him. Then, recalls Gallo, "he got right to the point. He said to me, 'listen, there's going to be a terrorist attack in New York. I can't tell you when, but we know it is going to happen and I cannot get any hospitals in the city to listen to me.' I said all right, 'I'll listen to you.' He said, 'look, we've been tracking these people for a long, long time, and we're getting a lot of intelligence that something's going to break, we just can't tell you when. Everybody has to pay attention and start planning now. These hospitals need to be prepared; it is going to be on a magnitude that this country has never seen before'."

Gallo was taken aback by O'Neill's prediction and intensity; by the idea of weapons of mass destruction striking New York. She was not sure exactly where this was going to go but she knew that she had to take O'Neill seriously. She told O'Neill she would go back and speak with Michael Dowling and figure out what to do. Gallo felt that with the nature of his job and experience, O'Neill had earned the right to be taken seriously. "I went back, I sat with Michael and I said, 'I don't know what we need to do, but we're going to have to do something'." Gallo was well aware that hospital systems were mandated by law to have disaster plans written up and she also knew that in most cases these plans were tucked away on a dusty shelf somewhere. O'Neill was lucky to have connected with Gallo. She had extensive experience in emergency medicine going back to her early days as a nurse. "There is nothing like working in that trauma room and having a patient come in by air or by ground and you're on one side of the universe trying to keep the patient here, and there is a force on other side of the universe trying to pull the patient over there," she says. "You never know what's coming through the door so you have to be prepared for anything and you try very hard to bring the patient to their optimal health status whatever that is. Then dealing with the families was always important for me. Life can change so quickly for people and in a trauma unit you see patients and families at the worst moments of their lives."

"We cannot believe that you are actually worried about a terrorist attack."

After meeting with John O'Neill, Gallo pulled together several of the Northwell emergency medical services experts including Gene Tangney and Brian O'Neill (no relation to John) and talked it through. Both Tangney and O'Neill had contacts on the New York City Fire Department and the city's office of emergency management, as well as in the office of then Mayor Rudolph Giuliani. After some discussion, Gallo and her colleagues created an educational program to build awareness throughout the Northwell system about threats posed by various potential disasters including terrorism. This was not something that was met with universal appreciation. "Most people went along with it," recalls Gallo, "but some people had the view that, 'yes, we know the standard disaster plans do not work, but we cannot believe that you are actually worried about a terrorist attack.' And I would say, 'well, I am making the grand leap that the FBI knows more than we do. And if we're wrong, well, we have a good system in place if we ever get an earthquake'."

Gallo and Dowling decided that in order to be really well prepared for a terrorist attack they needed to coordinate with

leading medical organizations in and around the city. The idea
was to build awareness of a potential threat and to see what
plans various organizations might collaborate on in anticipation of a threat, whatever it might be. Gallo and her team
organized and hosted a conference titled "Weapons of Mass
Destruction, Implications in Healthcare." In preparing for the
meeting, Gallo continued conversing with John O'Neill who
guided her on the type of gathering that might be helpful.
Gallo asked O'Neill to speak at the meeting and he agreed. As
they worked to build support for the meeting, the Northwell
team found that people from the New York Fire Department
as well as other public first-responders were eager to participate, as were public safety professionals from surrounding
areas including Westchester, Nassau, and Suffolk counties. The
conference agenda was not, however, high on the priority
list of major hospital and physician groups in New York City
and surrounding communities. Dowling made numerous calls
urging friends and colleagues from other health care organizations to join in. Some agreed, many did not. "Michael worked
the phones but we couldn't get any of the hospital CEOs to
come," recalls Gene Tangney. "Michael would say to them,
'hey, guys, this is really important'. It was disappointing to see
that many of our colleagues in health care leadership positions
were not appreciating the scale of the threat."

The meeting was set for mid-October, 2000, but it was
disrupted even before it started. Special Agent O'Neill, the
main speaker, was called to Yemen to investigate the terrorist
assault on the USS Cole, a guided-missile destroyer, attacked by
al-Qaeda while in a Yemeni port. Seventeen American sail-
ors were killed and 39 injured. O'Neill assured Gallo that in
his absence, he would arrange to have two colleagues[1] fill in
for him. The conference, designed to make health care leaders aware of the potential threat, kicked off with one of those
moments that, in retrospect, seems somehow surreal. The FBI
agent got up in front of the gathering and flashed a photograph
up on the screen. The health care professionals in the audience

looked up at the face on the screen and had no idea who he was. The agent said the country was at risk for a severe attack and "this is going to be the guy." The picture on the screen was of Osama bin Laden. This was October of 2000.

"What would we do if there was a terrorist attack?"

Gene Tangney was struck by the presentation. He felt as though he had been preparing his whole life to serve in conditions of disaster. Tangney was 15 years old when he first performed cardio-pulmonary resuscitation in an emergency situation. He was a medical explorer, a group similar to the Boy Scouts focused on young people interested in medicine and emergency services. Tangney worked for a number of years at Catholic Medical Center in Brooklyn and Queens as an Emergency Medical Technician responding to numerous disasters and high-profile events. He joined Northwell in 1997, where he worked under Kathy Gallo in the pre-hospital care division.

The New York meeting proved to be a defining moment for Tangney and the Northwell team. It was not that they were unaware of the dangers out there, but, as Tangney put it, the meeting "gave us an opportunity to focus on and appreciate the risks of the world we live in and we left there thinking we are a vital part of the emergency response infrastructure and that we had a lot of work to do to learn from others—whether from governments or global businesses. We left there with a sense of urgency and purpose." Yet somehow there had been a disconnect in the room. It seemed to Dowling, Gallo, and Tangney that a number of the other major health care organizations weren't taking the threat of terror all that seriously. For some people it seemed too far removed from the reality of life in New York. This was the United States, protected from the craziness in other parts of the world by vast oceans and the world's finest security forces. Perhaps for some the idea of domestic terrorism was too abstract. Perhaps with the bombing of the Cole 7,000 miles from New York City it seemed remote. The leaders of major hospitals in New York were largely focused internally, struggling each day to care for patients and remain financially stable. The natural tendency was to set terrorism lower on the agenda than other pressing concerns.

But for the Northwell folks, the threat, rather, *the need to prepare* for a threat, felt urgent. There was no need to wait to see whether there would be a terrible event. The responsibility was clear: Prepare well and quickly. "We really believed at the time that our health system had to become a leader in this area because nobody was doing it," recalls Tangney. "We started to discuss what would we do if there was a terrorist attack? A bomb? Nerve gas? If the lights go out? If we can't get gasoline? We started to develop an infrastructure around emergency preparedness and the beginning philosophy of an all-hazards approach. What are the skills and capabilities that we need? How do we prepare the system?"

Tangney and Brian O'Neill had many contacts throughout the emergency services world and they reached out to Walter Kowalczyk, who had worked for the FDNY emergency medical services division and was now a consultant specializing in emergency management. Working with Gallo, Tangney, and O'Neill, Kowalczyk helped put together a Network Incident Command structure within Northwell. This approach, then in use by first responders as well as the military, originated in the 1970s with a southern California coalition of firefighters and others seeking an effective management structure through which to fight forest fires. The existing response structure was too slow and cumbersome; too bureaucratic to respond appropriately to fast-moving events. Network Incident Command established clear lines of authority and empowered well-trained people to make in-the-moment judgments and take action in any sort of emergency. Embedding this structure within the Northwell system was no small matter. It involved time and effort to educate thousands of staff members throughout the system on the new approach. Northwell's commitment to the incident command structure deepened with the hiring of Jim Romagnoli, a 22 year veteran of the New York City Police Department where he worked as a detective in the emergency service unit, a group of specialists trained in the weapons and tactics needed to respond to a variety of emergency situations. His first day on the job at Northwell was September 1, 2001.

The core emergency services leadership team—Gallo, O'Neill, Tangney, and Romagnoli—created a hybrid model of emergency management. Many of the basics were already in place including, perhaps most importantly, a commitment from the top of the organization to build a world-class emergency capability. The team created a series of courses focused on aspects of incident command, particularly on teaching managers within the system how to think critically under duress. There was an initial reluctance on the part of doctors, nurses, and administrators who believed they were already well-prepared for emergencies. Some of the pushback was, *listen, we work in some of the most stressful conditions possible every day of the week.* But, over time, the substance of the teaching in the courses won people over. The kind of duress Romagnoli was talking about was an order of magnitude greater than what health care providers typically faced. "We teach them by putting them in different scenarios where the incident is growing minute-by-minute and they are suddenly thrust into an emergency," says Romagnoli. The training involves educating managers for both internal disasters—a fire within a hospital, for example—as well as external disasters such as acts of terrorism, airline crashes, etc. "We want them to learn to function in a compressed timeframe while under duress. In the simulation we take them down a road that always has forks in it so that a decision at one point may significantly narrow your options a few minutes later. It is important that they understand that in these kinds of situations they are never going to have all of the information or all of the tools they want so they have to be prepared to make a decision with 70 percent of the information they need."

"A willingness to take things that were outside of healthcare and bring them into healthcare."

Dowling and Gallo knew they were outliers. They knew that they were going more deeply into emergency preparedness than any of the other major health care systems in the greater New York area and they were comfortable with that for it aligned with their core values. Dowling thought of it this way: Northwell had a responsibility to do everything possible to provide quality care in clinics and hospitals, for births and end-of-life and everything in between. It also meant protecting people from the innumerable forces outside clinic and hospital walls—man-made disasters, acts of terror, acts of God. There was a sense of guardianship at work here; a belief that the mission was not just about healing the sick but about protecting the weak and vulnerable and in the face of catastrophic terrorism just about *everyone* was weak and vulnerable. Dowling and Mark Solazzo displayed a "willingness to take things that were not traditional in healthcare, things outside of healthcare and bring them into healthcare," says Tangney. "They believed that we had to be prepared for any emergency, that it was part of our social responsibility to be prepared and not just for our own patients and hospitals but for everyone." This idea of emergency management as a social responsibility is important to understanding the Northwell DNA and the real mission. "Emergency preparedness is about our hospitals and other facilities being ready and committed in the greatest times of need for our communities," says Solazzo. "We are a community asset and we are there for people as a safe haven."

In the fiercely competitive health care marketplace, patients make decisions about doctors and hospitals based on a variety of considerations. Reputation for quality is essential, of course, as is convenience. Patients do not generally choose a doctor or hospital based on its emergency management capability. Thus, it is an area where investing significant resources—people and dollars—is unlikely to yield any real return on investment, at least not measured in market share or financial return. It was clearly part of the mission, however, and in the realm of emergency management the Northwell mission impulse meshed with the organization's educational impulse. Just as Kathy Gallo had looked outside the health care industry for guidance in building the Center for Learning and Innovation, so too did the emergency team now look for help outside health care for emergency management. Global companies in manufacturing, financial services, and technology prepare for a variety of potential disasters including weather, political instability, cyber-attacks, and terrorism. Brian O'Neill met with leaders from MasterCard and PWC, the global consulting company, and exchanged thinking and strategies for best practices in managing crisis brought on by acts of terrorism. These companies had invested in planning and the security experts at those companies were knowledgeable about assessing and preparing for a variety of threats. Lessons from other industries proved valuable, but as Gallo and Tangney looked around they found few models for emergency preparedness within their own industry. "We had to create it ourselves and get the conversations going," says Gallo. "That's why we had that conference. We knew we couldn't do it by ourselves."

In addition to learning from private companies, the team drew lessons from contacts within the emergency medical services world—officials from the FDNY, the city's department of emergency services, the mayor's office. They wanted to fully understand the public emergency response system before building their own structure and discussions over time made clear the areas where the capabilities of hospitals, ambulances, physicians, nurses and others in the health care world could complement the network developed by first responders. With this "all hazards" approach in which their aspiration is to be prepared for any emergency with an adaptable command and response structure. "We can't close, we can't shut down," says Brian O'Neill. "People still have babies, people still have heart attacks and if you're not prepared, we've seen what it means. Your hospital closes because of Ebola and your staff gets sick. You have to evacuate your hospital during a storm. Those things cannot happen. There are basic things that you need to do in any disaster and if you really put them in place and you do a good job at it, you're able to rise to the occasion no matter what's coming at you."

An essential aspect of preparing for all hazards was building a first line of defense by assembling the largest fleet of ambulances in the region—mobile Intensive Care Units—staffed by 600 trained professionals, most of them paramedics. This capability exists for disaster response, of course, but it also provides Northwell's hospitals and clinics with a transport system that allows patients to be safely moved to the exact location within the system where they can get the best care. "Instead of having redundancy of capabilities in our hospitals, we have established centers of excellence focused on cardiac care, neuro-sciences, trauma, and behavioral health," says Tangney. "We have these centers of excellence which allows us to reduce duplication of services throughout the system. No matter what port of entry you come in, we can transport you to the right location for the right service at the right time in the right transport vehicle." This differs from hospitals where a patient is transported by an ambulance company with which they have a contract. Northwell hires and trains its own staff and thus, knows that each member of that staff is highly reliable as an advanced clinician. The idea is to provide the same level of clinical quality in transport as Northwell does within the system's hospitals. One of the complex challenges to emergencies involves duration. For first responders, such as fire and police, most disasters happen quickly and are over relatively quickly as well. Not so in health care where disasters may injure thousands of people and require months of treatment and hospitalization. "If you look at how municipalities handle emergencies, they're the first responders and we are the first receivers," says Romagnoli. "The casualties can stay with us for weeks or even months after the emergency situation is over."

"We thought we would be getting thousands of casualties."

On September 11, 2001, as images of the burning twin towers played out on the television screens, the GPS monitoring system inside the Northwell command center tracked the movement of every ambulance within the system. The emergency management team watched as 18 of those trucks converged on lower Manhattan. "We thought we would be getting thousands of casualties," Tangney recalls. While a few patients did appear at Staten Island University Hospital, there was nothing close to the numbers anticipated. "We were prepared in case all those casualties did show up. We used disciplines and methodologies that were proven—the incident command structure. We used all these different learnings to prepare ourselves for this day and we set up a control unit down there right next to it. One of the requests we got immediately was for surgical gloves. As much as we could find. We went everywhere to get them. The reason was they were picking up—every time they picked up a body part they had to get rid of the glove because it would contaminate—they couldn't pick up two body parts with the same glove."

Two days after the attacks Dowling and Mark Solazzo accompanied a team to the site. Dowling knew the area intimately having had an office on the 58th floor of 2 World Trade Center, where he had been just a week earlier for a day's worth of meetings. "It was smoldering," Dowling recalls. "Fires popping up all over the place. Unbelievably dangerous. It was absolutely astonishing and shocking to see what had just happened imagining that those buildings would come down. The thing I was amazed at was that everything that was in everybody's office files that everybody considered so important to their life was a foot deep in every street surrounding World Trade. It was a mass of paper files. You walk on top of them thinking this was somebody's big contract that, just days earlier, was the most important thing."

One of the saddest parts of all was when the Northwell team set up something akin to a field hospital at Chelsea Piers in Manhattan and it remained empty. No patients, painfully few survivors. The teams waited and waited and the surprise was hard to measure; the sense of bewilderment difficult to gauge. *How could this insane event have happened and there were no patients?* And soon enough the terrible truth about the extent of the devastation and loss of life emerged. A ray of light came from the story of Scott Strauss of the NYPD, who would later join Northwell, was later featured in the film *World Trade*, a story largely based on Scott's efforts to save a survivor in the depths of the rubble. Scott was in the bowels of the wreckage with the man trapped under a steel girder. Any shift in the massive pile could have crushed them, but Scott chose to remain with the injured man. After nine hours of effort, Scott freed him from the wreckage.

The events of 9/11 stand as the defining moment for the men and women whose professional lives are devoted to emergency services. Their world had changed forever. The sense that America was somehow apart or immune from the terror of the world vanished that day. It seemed that everyone at Northwell had friends who had died. Many lost family members. And the day after the attack, news came that FBI Special Agent John O'Neill himself had been inside his office at World Trade when the towers came down. It was all so tragic, so unthinkable, and there was a certain feeling of helplessness that there was nothing that anyone at Northwell could have done to mitigate the damage and loss of life. But for all the shock and sorrow in the aftermath of the attacks, it was clear that the Northwell team had been ready—as ready as you could be for a catastrophe of that magnitude; that Northwell had done what John O'Neill had asked; had taken him seriously and had worked to prepare for whatever was to come.

"Instead of disrupting the patients how about if we send you fuel?"

Everything changed after 9/11 and that included the sensibility of professionals in the emergency preparedness world. Emotions were raw for some time after the attack and there was a pervasive sense of grief that mixed uneasily with a determination to get back up and keep going. But there was also a wariness running throughout the emergency preparedness world. Suddenly in the United States, there was a new benchmark for disasters; a new definition of catastrophe, and it was, as John O'Neill had predicted to Kathy Gallo, an order of magnitude larger than anything the nation had ever before experienced. Barely 60 days after the twin towers came down, American Airlines flight 587, bound for Santo Domingo, took off from John F. Kennedy International Airport, then crashed into a Queens neighborhood killing all 260 passengers and crew as well as a number of people on the ground. The Northwell incident command was up and running upon news of the crash with a demonstration of readiness in hospitals, clinics, and throughout the ambulance service. Again, however, there were no survivors. In this instance investigators for the National Transportation Safety Board ruled within days of the crash that crew error, not terrorism, caused the crash. Pre-9/11, the crash of American 587 would have been an enormously important event and, for the families and loved ones of those killed, it surely was. In the broader community, however, there was a numbness brought on by 9/11; a wary anticipation that horrific things on a massive scale were in the offing. As with 9/11, however, the measure of the tragedy in one sense was that, again, even as Northwell's teams were at the ready, there were no patients to treat.

Less than two years later, with first responders still wary, the power grid in the Northeastern part of the United States failed. On a steamy day in August of 2003, the blackout affected eight states in the Northeast into the Midwestern part of the country and constituted the worst blackout ever in the U.S. Every hospital in the Northwell system lost power went into incident command mode. Every backup generator at Northwell facilities kicked in on cue, except one, and there were contingency plans that enabled an additional generator to be brought on line right away. All of the contingencies had been rehearsed in advance. Part of the preparation also included agreements with a variety of vendors—including those selling fuel to Northwell—that the pipeline would remain open under any and all circumstances. During the blackout, backup generators kicked in at virtually all major hospitals but these generators depended upon large quantities of fuel to operate and within hours some hospitals were running dangerously low and unable to identify a source of resupply. "We had baked into our plan long before the blackout that fuel would be there for us," recalls Kathy Gallo. "We received a call from a big hospital in Queens asking whether we could take their ICU patients. They were blacked out and about to run out of fuel, and I said, 'instead of disrupting the patients how about if we send you fuel?' and that's what we did."

"How sure are you the storm will hit New York?"

It was late October, 2012, Tropical Storm Sandy moved steadily up the east coast of the United States and, as it did so, the threat to the New York area grew more ominous. Monitoring storms of consequence is an essential part of the work at the emergency preparedness center and this low pressure system captured the attention not only of the team but of the organization's senior leaders, Dowling and Solazzo, about ten days before it struck. The original forecasts called for the storm to veer off the coast and head out to sea, sparing the northeastern part of the United States. Notwithstanding that prediction, it was difficult not to pay attention to the storm given its sheer enormity. The emergency center protocols pre-scribe specific actions—equipment moved to staging areas five days out, contingency staffing plans adjusted two days out, etc. As the storm lumbered up the coast, the possibility increased that it could strike the New York area with extreme force. While there is no way of knowing when an external event such as an act of terror might strike, other events, including hurricanes, are predictable to some extent. "With a hurricane I know it's coming and shame on me if I am not ready for it," says Romagnoli. As the storm moved north, tension among the team members built. There was concern about the possible damage to the system, but also concern about making the right call—to close hospitals, or not, whether to move patients. These were potentially life-threatening decisions difficult under ideal circumstances made more so given the uncertainty over the storm's path. Gallo, O'Neill, Romagnoli, and Tangney worked at gathering and analyzing data and discussed options, but the final call on what to do fell to Dowling and Solazzo. It became clearer each passing hour that there would be a significant threat to two of Northwell's facilities—Staten Island University Hospital and Southside Hospital in Bay Shore, Long Island. The question was whether to evacuate those facili-ties. Doing so would present significant risks to patients. *Not* doing so could be even riskier. As decision-time approached, Dowling and Solazzo asked the team members, *how sure are you the storm will hit New York? Very sure*, they said. And thus, the decision was made to evacuate 1100 patients—some gravely ill—and move them to other locations. Evacuating a hospital is the last resort. A year before, with Hurricane Irene, many hospitals in the New York area had been evacuated when, in hindsight, few, if any, evacuations were required. It made the judgment with Sandy more difficult. Making that call 48 hours out meant there was a chance that the storm would turn out to sea and the evacuations would not have been needed. But Dowling and Solazzo were convinced by the team's information and analysis that the safest route for patients was to evacuate. They had an emergency evacuation plan in place. Moving 1100 patients from two hospitals would be both extremely expensive and dangerous. Much could go wrong with any given transport from one hospital to another, particularly with really sick patients. Multiply that risk times a thousand and the concern for patient safety was real. Flooding and the loss of electrical power were threats to all patients—those in the ICUs, certainly, as well as any patient dependent upon any kind of mechanical device; that is to say, virtually every patient in both hospitals. There was another complicating factor: The evacuation had to be completed 48 hours *before* the storm made landfall when winds had not yet reached sustained velocity of 40 miles per hour. At that level, regulations prevent ambulances from traveling across major bridges for fear of windblown accidents. At nine feet high with a flat surface, ambulances are essentially a mobile ICU atop a truck chassis. Exposure on a high bridge to powerful winds invited disaster.

The evacuation required transferring each patient to exactly the right setting for the condition affecting them. Burn patients, for example, had to be transferred to a burn unit, ICU patients to another intensive care unit, labor and delivery patients to a labor and delivery setting, etc. Thousands of staff members began the process by identifying patients who could be rapidly discharged, and those patients who would be stable at home with their medications. The entire event was choreographed from a central emergency operations center where assignments and areas of responsibility are clearly defined. The decisions on where to send patients and how to transport them were based on how critical their condition was, the exact type of facility they needed to go to, and the level of transport required to move them safely. Some patients could travel in a regular ambulance with a normal staff level while others required fully staffed advanced life support ambulances.

"We absorbed all of those patients within our system, moving all of them to another Northwell facility," says Tangney. Southside and Staten Island hospitals remained open throughout the storm period with skeleton crews to care for people in emergencies—accidents, new babies, etc. Neither hospital ever closed. "We never went down, ever, and other institutions around us were folding left and right," recalls Tangney. Other organizations relied upon the Northwell emergency management capability to evacuate their hospitals and nursing homes. By October 27, the major New York area airports were shut down as were the main railroad lines, several bridges, and tunnels. Sections of the city as well as portions of some towns on Long Island were evacuated. At the height of the storm, generators at the New York University Langone Medical Center failed requiring the evacuation of hundreds of patients.

Mission

At Northwell there is a particular sensitivity to monitoring the existence and scope of infectious diseases no matter where in the world they might exist. Northwell's proximity to three large international airports—JFK, LaGuardia, and Newark—place major points of entry to the U.S. within minutes of Northwell hospitals. A passenger arriving from Asia with bird flu, or one traveling from Africa with symptoms of Ebola, could well arrive on the Northwell doorstep. When the first Ebola case presented in Texas, Northwell was already on alert, but as Tangney notes, the case revealed that it was essential to have all clinical personnel able to identify possible symptoms. "When we first heard about it in Texas we went into emergency management mode where we re-evaluated protocols based on the presentation of that patient," he says. "It was a huge learning experience for all of us. We had to change the way we identify infectious diseases. It meant increasing surveillance to a new level. We reviewed our policies and all access points into our system needed to be catalogued. And a protocol was put in place for how to identify and isolate patients who were possibly infected. All employees had to be trained to identify the symptoms. The ability to recognize and isolate the disease was our best defense."

Training thousands of staff members to be able to identify and diagnose the disease was one challenge. The next was building a capability to treat Ebola patients and that meant establishing protocols that allowed clinicians to treat patients but at the same time protected clinicians from the virus. From an emergency management standpoint Ebola required per-fection. The virus is so lethal that even a miniscule mistake could lead to the infection not only of doctors, nurses and other caregivers, but could also potentially spread throughout the population. When the Ebola alarm sounded worldwide, Mark Solazzo along with Tangney and Gallo convened a team of emergency experts and other clinicians—more than 100 people in all—and worked to prepare for what was a threat-ened disaster. Two weeks later the team was ready to receive patients, should the need arise (Part of the preparation process involved creating a detailed manual for how to prepare for and deal with Ebola. The manual has since been downloaded by organizations throughout the world hundreds of times). For months after the initial case in Texas, Tangney and his colleagues continued training and retraining staff members through the Center for Learning and Innovation. At the same time, a team worked to design and develop protocols for the use of protective garments for clinicians who would be treat-ing Ebola patients. Doctors and nurses created a specialty care unit at Glen Cove Hospital capable of treating any Ebola patient who might arrive at any Northwell facility. "Ebola was different, and actually, it was exciting from a program devel-opment point of view, because it was not just about acquir-ing knowledge," says Tangney. "Yes, it is important that they understood Ebola from a disease standpoint, but the difference in that program from all others was the intensive focus on personal protective equipment. Getting in and out of those hazmat suits is *critical.* For the Ebola teams there's a total of eighty-four hours of training. There was online education for knowledge acquisition and then once the Ebola unit was set up in Glen Cove, we actually bought simulators and put them up there so that they could learn in the environment that they would be working in. It is just very, very different because here you have those that volunteered, the Ebola team risking their lives and we took that very seriously that we were part-nering with them to give them the skillset to stay safe. During training when somebody was taking off the suit incorrectly we had to stop, timeout right away, everybody freeze. It was labor intensive, resource intensive." As the federal government issued a series of constantly shifting guidelines, the Northwell team decided to opt for suits that would afford employees the highest possible level of protection—level III hazmat suits. At one point during the period of preparation, a *New York Times* photographer visited the unit and took pictures of a doctor wearing the protective clothing the team had designed. It so happened that the photograph was published on the front page of the *Times* shortly before a congressional hearing con-cerning the dangers of the disease. Some members of the con-gressional committee were concerned that guidance from the Centers for Disease Control had been insufficiently detailed or even contradictory. During the course of the televised hearing a member of congress interviewing the head of the CDC held up the *Times* and showed the Northwell protocol as an exam-ple of how clinicians should be dressed.

"I think Ebola really validated us as an organization," says Tangney. "It was when you saw the hospital in Texas go down, it was such a scary thing and Michael vowed never to let that happen in this health system and we not only rose to the occasion but we became a leader in how to react to the disease. We're sitting ten miles from JFK and we agreed to become one of the central receivers of Ebola patients. We created a unit within weeks to handle it validated by the CDC. We didn't *have* to do any of that. We wanted to do it. It's part of our mission."

Endnote

1. Special Agents PatD'Amuro and Bill Zinnikas.

Chapter 6

What Does Quality Care Look Like?

"We are there to take care of him, part of his support system. We want to build that relationship because otherwise he could easily fall through the cracks."

Dr. Mariecel Pilapil

If you Google the phrase *quality health care* you get 547 million hits in a half second, exceeding by more than 200 million the number of hits for the phrase *great sex.* The idea of quality in health care is ubiquitous—the industry's Holy Grail. Every organization involved in any way with the industry seeks to contribute, in some way, to achieving quality care. But what, exactly, is quality care? What does it look like? What are its essential components? Definitions of quality most often cited come from the Institute of Medicine—that quality is "the degree to which health care services for individuals and populations increase the likelihood of desired health outcomes and are consistent with current professional knowledge." The United States Agency for Healthcare Research and Quality defines quality as "doing the right thing for the right patient, at the right time, in the right way to achieve the best possible results."

These are excellent definitions, and while these views of quality from 30,000 feet are important, it is also useful to view quality at ground level and when we do so we see the reality at the front lines; a care delivery process that is often untidy, messy, frequently chaotic, and hit-or-miss. So what does quality care look like on the front lines? Not in the suite of an elite academic medical center with a world-renowned specialist, but in the clinic with the neediest of patients suffering from multiple complex chronic conditions often including behavioral health challenges? In a clinic where the waiting area and every exam room are full?

Quality is not any one thing. It is a recipe of varied elements, ingredients that, when skillfully mixed together, produce the magic brew. What are those ingredients? It is a long list but in this chapter we focus on core elements. Measurement, for example, is essential to quality, as is transparency of data. Trust is a core element of quality for we know that trusting relationships between caregivers and patients make for better outcomes. Physician satisfaction—and the satisfaction levels of all providers—is an often overlooked element of quality. Value (the combination of quality and cost) goes hand-in-hand with quality. To really understand quality we need to begin at ground level, at the front lines of care where quality is as obvious in some cases as it is elusive in others.

Caring for Vincent

Late in 2016, Dr. Mariecel Pilapil and her team gathered in their Great Neck, Long Island, clinic for their morning huddle. Dr. Pilapil sat in a cramped office surrounded by her team members: Two resident physicians in training; a clinical pharmacist with a PhD along with a clinical pharmacy student in training; and a medical assistant who coordinated many of the appointments. The team's behavioral health specialist was with a patient at that time. Led by Dr. Pilapil, the team members reviewed the day's roster of patients that embody the challenge in health care all across the United States today.

Sixty-eight year old female, Spanish speaking, was on a statin, not clear if she is still taking it.

Thirty-four year old female, poorly controlled diabetes, bladder issue, depression, prior suicide attempts.

Thirty-one year old male, significantly overweight, poorly controlled diabetes, severe infections in feet which nearly required amputation; scrotal abscess and genital warts; will not allow doctors to examine; missed numerous prior appointments.

Fifty-two year old female, history of ovarian cancer, up to date on all screenings; panic attacks, physical abuse in the home (husband now moved out); two teenaged sons, worries how to survive financially; needs treatment for toenail infection.

And then there is Vincent: *Sixty year old, unmarried man, lives alone, diabetes, hypertension, coronary artery disease, learning disabilities (dropped out of high school after sustained mockery from other students); two heart attacks, two stents implanted; says he is taking his medication but seems clear that he is not. Blood pressure this morning 180/100.*

"The first thing we do is triage what needs to be addressed immediately and what can wait," says Dr. Pilapil. She and her team are dealing in a realm not of perfection, but of the possible. Quality care is often about choices; about what is possible to do in the moment. While Vincent is due for a colonoscopy and other screenings, the fact that his blood pressure is so high means he is at risk of stroke and heart attack "so we focus on that as opposed to doing a colonoscopy screening," she says. "You cannot address all things in one visit so we triage what needs to be done first."

Vincent embodies the quality/cost challenge in health care. A Commonwealth Fund analysis[1] of care delivered to high-need patients found that "in any given year, 10 percent of patients account for 65 percent of the nation's health care expenditures. Moreover, many high-need patients (with two or more major chronic conditions such as diabetes or heart failure), also have unmet social needs that may exacerbate their medical conditions." The study found that "the health care system is currently failing to meet the complex needs of these patients" and that "high-need patients have greater unmet behavioral health and social issues than do other adults and require greater support to help manage their complex medical and nonmedical requirements. Results indicate that with better access to care and good patient–provider communication, high-need patients are less likely to delay essential care and less likely to go to the emergency department for non-urgent care, and thus less likely to accrue avoidable costs."[2]

A major portion of Vincent's health is determined not by what Dr. Pilapil and her team members do (or fail to do), but by what Vincent eats and whether he exercises; by his income, quality of housing, social connections; on all of the social determinants of health traditionally beyond the scope of what doctors worried about. That has changed. The pursuit of health means doctors push to try to influence as many of the social determinants as they can. It is, to be sure, an uphill struggle. "Quality outcomes depend not only on what providers do, but also on community support that can be leveraged to assure good outcomes," says Dr. Mark Jarrett. "It is difficult to expect people to worry about whether they smoke or not if they cannot pay the rent and utilities. We need to focus more on these things and less on the hospital world."

This is an enormous challenge. It is difficult for caregivers to get their arms around these patients in large measure because much of what harms their health has little to do with what happens in clinic and, in fact, is dependent upon lifestyle choices involving poor nutrition, alcohol, tobacco, and drugs, and a variety of other "social determinants of health" that lie well outside the clinic. The good news is that there are people like Mariecel Pilapil and her team devoting their professional lives to solving this most difficult and urgent health care challenge. Dr. Pilapil is 32 years old, a cum laude graduate of Harvard who earned her medical degree at Mount Sinai School of Medicine in Manhattan where she focused on both internal medicine and pediatrics. She joined Northwell in 2013 right out of her residency and she cares for adult and pediatric patients while at the same time supervising residents. This clinic in which she works, at 865 Northern Blvd in Great Neck, Long Island, serves as a patient-centered medical home[3] for thousands of patients. The idea is to provide a clinical home where patients know they can go, see people they trust who know them, and get whatever care they need. This clinic, the largest single primary care practice within Northwell Health, includes 20 doctors and more than a hundred additional clinical and administrative personnel. As Dr. Pilapil's team gathers around in a circle, laptops open, coffee cups in hand, the discussion gets focused quickly: What drugs might best control Vincent's blood pressure? They discuss the pros and cons in a highly technical back and forth before deciding upon a mix of medications. Having clinical pharmacists as part of the primary care team—certainly not the standard everywhere—makes a significant difference, says Pilapil. An extraordinary amount of time, thought, and effort goes into deciding which medications patients should receive and at which doses. In clinic, it sometimes seems that piecing together the medications puzzle for patients can take up as much or more time than anything else. "The pharmacists we work with have PhD degrees, they are very, very experienced," she says. "By far the biggest thing that has changed my practice from Mount Sinai where I trained has been working with pharmacists. They are an incredible resource for medication management, adjusting medications, ideas for patients with diabetes and what medications to start them on. It is really helpful to have them sit down with a patient and go over their medications with them and discuss the side effects and make sure patients are taking medications."

"We want to build that relationship because otherwise he could easily fall through the cracks."

While there are many similarities among patients that she and her team see, Pilapil notes that every patient is unique and that it is important to understand the context of each patient's life. Family support for patients can make a difference especially when it comes to faithfully taking medications, but Vincent doesn't have such support, "so we try and work around that by figuring out ways to remind him about taking his medication and coming to his appointments. We can prescribe medications, but if he is not taking them or there are other barriers to taking them then we look at the logistics and try and address those issues. If cost is an issue we can help with that. Our pharmacists are good at finding deals. We make sure that we do everything we can to enable him to come to appointments so that if he cannot come Monday at 9 a.m. because of work then we find time he would be able to come that would work for him."

Pilapil and her team make it their business to pay attention to "everything that follows after he leaves" his appointment including transportation, pharmacy needs, and appointments with specialists. There are moments in clinic when it feels as though the job here is not unlike that of the air traffic control team at nearby JFK International Airport. In clinic, the team members strive to stay current, keep up with the unending patient flow in an effort to keep all those patients up and going and make sure nobody crashes. Vincent's cognitive deficits are such that he may not be able "to convey the reason we are sending him to a specialist because maybe his level of understanding is not there for him to be able to communicate with a specialist." During the course of this particular day, Pilapil explains that they would like to do some additional testing to get his medications calibrated and his blood pressure under control. Vincent, however, is devoted to his job and worried about being late. He asks whether one of the residents, Dr. Amanda Simone, might call his boss. Simone pulls out her cell phone and does just that, explaining the situation to Vincent's boss and asking whether it is okay for him to be late. Absolutely says the boss and Vincent is very pleased indeed. These types of requests—call a parent, adult child, sibling, others—are common and Dr. Pilapil and her colleagues do their best to fulfill them.

"Getting Vincent's diabetes and blood pressure under control would be big," she says. "We are trying to build a relationship with him where we are there to take care of him, part of his support system. We want him to know that if he has a concern he can contact us and see us. We want to build that relationship because otherwise he could easily fall through the cracks." Along with quality, the major concern in healthcare in the United States involves cost so it is reasonable to wonder what the cost of the care on this day was for Vincent. Dr. Pilapil did not know the cost on the day of Vincent's clinic visit but she was informed by the clinic's billing department that under Medicaid this visit, (considered a follow-up), yielded a grand total in revenue for Northwell Health of $125.

The pursuit of quality is an ideal, of sorts—*the right care at the right time in the right setting at the right place.* And it would be uplifting to say that this definition of quality is met most of the time but it would also be disingenuous. Vincent, for example, was scheduled for a follow-up two weeks later to check his blood pressure, but he did not show up. Pilapil's team reached out to him and set up another appointment a couple of weeks later and he did show up for that. "At that visit, he was actually able to tell us all of his medications and doses incorporating the changes we had advised him to make at his earlier visit," says Pilapil. "This was a significant improvement in terms of how well he seemed to know his meds. His blood pressure, however, was still quite a bit above goal. During the visit, while inquiring about his dietary choices, Dr. Simone uncovered that he had actually been eating three to four times a week" at a national burger and fries chain. "During the visit, Amanda pulled up the menu on her laptop while in the room with him and went through each of the things he regularly eats at that establishment and explained why they were not good for his blood pressure, diabetes, etc. She suggested some 'healthier' options like the grilled fish or grilled chicken, though still not ideal. He's supposed to follow up in five weeks."

Training as a Team, Working as a Team

Pilapil's boss, Dr. Joseph Conigliaro, serves as Chief of General Internal Medicine at Northwell, a position from which he oversees care for tens of thousands of patients like Vincent. During the 29 years he has worked as a physician, Dr. Conigliaro, a graduate of Harvard Medical School, has learned some basic lessons about quality care and among the most important is that, as a general rule, teams deliver better care than individuals. A coordinated team distributes the burden of work among members based on varying skills. So what does quality care *look like*? It looks like a team. Having a clinical pharmacist on the primary care team, for example, as noted with Dr. Pilapil's team, solves medication issues in the moment. A few years ago, Conigliaro started to think about how caregivers were trained. If the route to better quality is having clinicians practice together in teams, he thought, wouldn't it also make sense for those same clinicians to *train* together in teams? That, however, was not the tradition. For generations, doctors, nurses, pharmacists and others trained within their own professional silos. Conigliaro and his colleagues created a new approach which was manifest in the way Dr. Pilapil and her team worked and trained together. "In the old model the doctor practices in isolation and the rest of the people are support or ancillary staff," says Conigliaro. He is developing a new approach in the clinic where Pilapil and her associates are located. With this approach, the caregivers who are in their training phase—resident physicians, nurses, pharmacists, physician assistants, and others—are together throughout much of the work day. All the trainees get their own individual attention, which is the old model, but they also interact with each other and in doing so, gain a deeper understanding of their teammate's view of the patient's world. The idea is to learn to work as well-coordinated teams for the benefit of patients.

"We are training residents, students, physician assistants, pharmacists, and psychologists together so that when they go out into the work force they know how to work together," says Conigliaro. "We train them together because this is how they work. Also prominent on the team are the medical assistant and the medical secretary. They know the patients as well. I have 12 patients today including let's call her Mrs. Jones coming in at two. I work with my medical assistants who know she is due for her yearly mammogram, so when I huddle with team members we discuss each case. She is diabetic so she will need to have her blood tested to see where she is with regard to her diabetes. Let us make sure that I do not forget and we have the request ready to go. My medical assistant who will actually know all this will get that done ahead of time. This way it is not all on me. If you anticipate some of this stuff, when I go in to see the patient it has already been done. It makes me much more efficient and makes sure I do not miss anything." The increasingly collaborative nature of care delivery is not only desirable but necessary. Fewer medical students than ever are choosing primary care as their preferred career path as other specialties offer a less harried, better paid professional life. Thus, scarce face time with physicians grows scarcer still.

Many things in health care are difficult to measure and one of those is that most precious of elements—trust. Conigliaro sees trust between patient and doctor, between patient and team, as essential in pursuit of quality. Quality care comes from "having your own primary care provider that you actually see often enough that you know who that person is and they know you," he says. "You know that *they are a team* so you feel comfortable with their medical assistant and it is usually the same medical assistant, the same nurse, and the same phlebotomist." Developing a trusting relationship with patients requires the care team to think from the patient's perspective about access and convenience—clinic hours and appointment times matters to all patients but perhaps particularly to patients whose lives are under stress from family, work, or financial issues. A primary care team that accommodates a patient's schedule—where early morning, evening, or weekend appointments are available to suit the patient—affords the kind of access that improves quality while building trust. A trusting relationship builds the kind of confidence where patients do not hesitate to raise any and all issues with their doctor. "If we have a relationship of trust you are more likely to divulge things to me," says Conigliaro. "If I am not judgmental and my team is not judgmental I am more likely to get that information out of you. A lot of times my patients come and they apologize to me and say, 'I do not mean to bother you, but I am really just worried.' This actually makes my job easier. If you come in now for something that is very minimal, that is much better for your health and makes my job easier. If you come in eight months from now then this will be something that could be really significant, you have made it much harder for yourself and made it more complicated and difficult to treat you and get you well."

"I never label them because then they get defensive."

Among the main determinists of poor health are alcohol, tobacco, and recreational drugs. Conigliaro applies a simple screening device that seeks to identify potential problems in these areas before they spin out of control. As part of routine care, Conigliaro's teams ask a series of five questions[4] of all patients to determine whether there is an issue with alcohol, drugs, or tobacco.

- In the past 12 months have you used drugs other than those required for medical reasons?
- How often do you have a drink containing alcohol?
- How many drinks containing alcohol do you have on a typical day of drinking?
- How often do you have six or more drinks on one occasion?
- During the past year how often have you used tobacco products?

When a patient screens positive the medical assistant informs a behavioral health coach and the doctor then has a follow-up discussion with the patient. "We ask whether the patient has more than four drinks in a week and that is enough to start a conversation," says Conigliaro. "We discuss it and remind patients what defines safe drinking and their limit of four per week is within the safety guidelines. But let's say with another patient it's 17 drinks a week and you have six on Friday night. That is clearly hazardous drinking. The guidelines [from the National Institute of Alcoholism and Alcohol Abuse define safe drinking as 14 or fewer per week for men and seven or fewer per week for women]. You may not be dependent or an alcoholic but at that level of drinking you are more likely to get in a wreck, get in a fight, or develop a chronic problem with your liver or pancreas. You binge on Friday nights, Saturdays and Sundays; but you are able to wake up and go to work. If I recognize your behavior early on, there is data that shows that a simple counseling session by your provider or in your doctor's office motivates people to cut down. The research has shown that if you screen in primary care you are more likely to uncover it. When we deal with it in primary care we can help change behavior so the patient doesn't need to go to an addiction specialist or treatment center."

In teaching medical and nursing students as well as other members of the care team, Conigliaro makes the point that just as it is essential to make an early diagnosis concerning a patient's diabetes or elevated cholesterol, so, too, is it essential to make the earliest possible diagnosis of a patient who has a drug or alcohol problem. For the approach to work, it also must be clear that responsibility for changing behavior lies fully with the patient. Conigliaro and his team members are there to help and advise, but success depends upon a commitment from the patient. "I do not force you to do anything. The responsibility is yours," Conigliaro tells patients. "What do you want to do about it?"

In many cases patients are not ready to make a change until they are fully aware that their habit lies outside normal, healthy behavior. Some patients are unmoved, of course, and continue along a self-destructive path, but many patients begin to make changes. "I never label them," says Conigliaro, "because then they get defensive. I do not say, 'you are an alcoholic and you need to stop drinking.' It is important to take away the stigma and defensiveness so that patients are more receptive to a discussion." He will ask whether a patient is aware that he is drinking more than about 90 percent of the male population in that patient's age group. "I will say, 'I am really concerned about the amount that you drink in a week and given that you have high blood pressure and reflux disease your alcohol is actually making that worse.' A patient will say, 'instead of having three beers a night I will have two beers a night. I will just stop at two. That is pretty doable.' The patient comes back after a while and their blood pressure is a little lower and they have put two and two together and now their reflux is better. And now, hopefully, we have prevented them from having a really major adverse event."

There are, of course, many patients who need more than a nudge to change their behavior and when a patient presents with a significant problem with alcohol or drugs, Conigliaro does a "warm handoff," personally introducing the patient to a behavioral health specialist. This makes it more likely that the patient will take the next step—that is, engage with the behavioral health specialist and work through whatever treatment or coaching is most suitable. "We work closely with health coaches who are very skilled at helping patients stop drinking or cut down on drinking," he says, "and that is something primary care doctors never used to do."

"We intervened early and hopefully prevented significant deterioration."

Nowhere is the pursuit of quality care more challenging or more elusive than with behavioral health. The evolution of our society during just the past few decades has been remarkable in many positive ways, yet the trend in mental and behavioral health is disturbing. Every day Drs. Conigliaro and Pilapil and their colleagues face challenges from patients who present with an array of behavioral health issues ranging from problem drinking to mental illness to threats of suicide. "When a patient with diabetes or congestive heart failure or any number of issues also has depression, anxiety, or schizophrenia, providing consistent care becomes much more challenging," says Conigliaro. Historically, treatment for medical issues such as diabetes exists in one silo while treatment for mental health issues resides in another silo. This division is anything but patient-centered. Integrating the two has proven to be clearly in the overall interest of patients' health and well-being. It has become clear over time that doing so in a primary care setting, while by no means easy, can help. This is an area of particular interest for government agencies, Medicaid in particular, which pays for coverage of people who tend to have multiple complex chronic conditions including behavioral health issues. The federal government has created incentives, administered by the states, to help doctors redesign their practices to integrate behavioral health capabilities into primary care more effectively. This program has helped Conigliaro and his colleagues establish teams of health coaches available to patients by telephone. The coaches help guide patients by answering their questions and steering them to the appropriate type of care depending upon their condition. "Often times patients don't need care from the Emergency Room but they don't know that," says Conigliaro. "Health coaches help them understand the best options." In some instances coaches connect the patient with the pharmacists for a medication adjustment, while in others, the coach sets up an appointment for the patient with a doctor or nurse in clinic.

"The real revolution is that quality is now looked at as something measureable."

The pursuit of quality, in Conigliaro and Pilapil's clinics or anywhere else, is inextricably linked to measurement. It was not so very many years ago that doctors were rarely graded on anything after medical school or training. In retrospect, it seems odd. Among the brightest people in society, doctors are traditionally more than comfortable being tested and graded from childhood through their late 20s or early 30s when the grading ends abruptly. No longer. In health care now the grading for physicians never ends. Dr. Ira Nash, senior vice president and Executive Director of Northwell Health Physician Partners, the umbrella for all physicians employed by the health system, makes an important point suggesting that "the reason why we traditionally went from 'hyper-grading' in college and med school to 'no grading' in clinical training and practice is that until relatively recently, no one believed that one could measure clinical quality in a meaningful way. The real revolution is that quality is now looked at as something measurable." Reasonable people can argue the merits of this approach, but the reality is that in a consumer-centric world where just about every product and service is rated by consumers online, the same is happening in health care. While many physicians are justifiably concerned with posting individual ratings—these things are inherently complex—there is also a growing recognition among physicians that in the new, data-rich world, disclosure of physician ratings was inevitable.

The notion of measurable standards for quality became an important part of the Northwell culture starting back in the mid-1990s when Abraham Krasnoff, then a trustee at North Shore University Hospital, established a performance improvement coordinating group. Among Mark Solazzo's first assignments upon arriving at Northwell was to staff this committee and he recalls that "when any new hospital would come into the system the Krasnoff committee was there to help guide the new clinical teams. When there would be some kind of quality issue such as a medical error, Abraham Krasnoff and the committee members would basically say, 'let's talk about how we can learn from that.' We made clear that ours was not a *gotcha* culture, but that it was a culture of safety and learning." A key player on the committee was Yosef Dlugacz, PhD, an authority on quality management in health care. The evidence-based approach advocated by Krasnoff, Dlugacz, Solazzo, and the other committee members, was the kind of analysis that doctors could accept.

"The ground has been prepared for this effort by the fact that people see all around them that everything is getting rated," says Nash. "I said from the beginning that 'this isn't about whether you want to be rated or not, this is about whether you want Yelp to do it or Health Grades to do it or Vitals or Web MD or whatever—sites over which you have no control and there's not even a connection necessarily between the people who are writing those reviews and the people who are seeing our doctors." Nash has solved that problem by developing a transparent process where "only our patients who have actually seen us, get a survey." Nash was careful about the pace at which he moved the disclosure process forward, pacing it in stages so that the physicians would be comfortable (enough) and that the goal of transparency would be served. "We now publish on our own website the patient experience scores and comments that patients provide through Press Ganey, our third party vendor," he says. "I used to joke that I was going to get a remote starter for my car when we first launched this and I think in retrospect we did a number of things that really made it less contentious and less controversial by the time we actually turned it on than it would have been. The first is that we had a very long and deliberate process to get to the point where we went public. It was really two years before that that we started working on this to build both the infrastructure to do it and to make it culturally acceptable to do it." Nash's first step was to provide individual physicians with measures of their own performance. "We created a score-card that every doc got emailed to him or her directly, 'Here are your scores. Here's how to compare it to everybody in your department. Here's how you compare to a national sample of people who practice in your discipline and here's how you're tracking over time'." These scores were seen only by the indi-vidual physician and his or her clinical leader. After a period of time, Nash upped the ante and results of individual physician scores were published on an internal intranet site accessible to any clinician within a given practice. This was eye-opening. Now every doctor could see how he or she compared on important measures to colleagues in similar practices.

But public reporting was always the goal and, toward that end, Nash assembled a committee of physicians to plan how to get to that point. "I wanted some cover to make this some-thing that the group could own and not feel like this was being imposed upon them," he says, "so I sent out a message to all our membership asking for volunteers for the group and I had it in the back of my mind that some people were going to volunteer for this group to sabotage the process. I made it clear that we were recruiting people for this committee with the idea that they would be charged with figuring out how we were going to publicly report this and what rules would we follow. So I knew there would be people who would volunteer with the idea of 'I'm going to see to it that this is never done.' And so when it came time to pick the chair of the commit-tee I went to that website and I looked at everybody's patient experience scores to make sure that the person I picked was somebody who was actually good at this and committed to this and she's been great. And so the committee first met in the beginning of 2015 and created a set of rules about how we were going to do this, how many surveys do you need to have, what kind of comments will get posted, what kind won't, what's the appeals process, how will this look?"

Predictably, there was pushback. *My patient population is unusually difficult and oh by the way I don't like the way you measured.* This was fairly common but once it was demonstrated that the measurements were reliable, this sort of criticism grew more muted. Dr. Conigliaro, for one, embraced Nash's push for measurement. "It's not meant to be punitive because it's about improvement," says Conigliaro. "There is a certain level that we want everybody to be. The reason we share everyone's data is so that people who are not performing as well can go to the higher performers and ask, 'how do you do this exactly? What do you do that makes this work so well?' We compare practices in order to improve. It's not about embarrassing anyone. It's about giving better patient care. We all meet quarterly and everybody's practice is displayed. We know that XYZ's practice is the best and ABC's practice is the worst. What we do is it is not to shame them. It is to have those performing at a lower level learn from the more successful practices."

Dr. Kris Smith, medical director of Advanced Illness Management, makes an important observation. "The wonderful thing about physicians," he says, "is when they see that the guy over there is out-performing them they're serving as a model for the rest of the organization and like, 'wow Lenox Hill is doing this, we should be able to do it too.' And so there's really a momentum that picks up because everybody fundamentally wants to do a great job taking care of their patients."

"The dirty little secret about all of this is that most patients really like their doctor."

There is an important provision that helps take some of the sting out of the transparency. Doctors are notified when any new comment about them comes into the website and they then have an opportunity to review and challenge any of the comments. If a comment is somehow inappropriate (with false claims or a personal attack, for example) there is an internal peer-review process and, if necessary, comments can be blocked. As of early 2017, more than 19,000 comments had been posted for over 1000 different doctors. Only a few dozen (44) of those comments have been flagged and challenged by physicians. "So the dirty little secret about all of this," says Nash, "is that most patients really like their doctor and so the concern that our physicians had before we went live with this has just not been borne out by the data that we're getting back, with very rare exceptions."

Physician grades from Press Ganey Co., which are ubiquitous throughout the world of health care, are important markers for Northwell doctors. Press Ganey sends surveys to patients after they have seen their doctor or had another type of encounter with a health system. The interviews are by mail, and on the web. These reports can take weeks or even months to gather, process, and deliver. Dr. Mark Jarrett, Chief Quality Officer for Northwell, wants more real-time data to push for learning and improvement. "Getting performance data in real-time is important to performance improvement," he says. There is something particularly powerful about real time data that gets physicians to take it more seriously, even more personally, he says. "Culturally real-time data gets people to think, 'these are not just numbers—this is somebody's grandmother, or somebody's mother, or somebody's sister, or brother, or child.' That is important if you are going to develop a really and truly highly reliable organization. Because people have to think about everything they are doing and are they doing it the right way and not cutting corners. If they get fixated on report cards, then they do not think about it the right way."

In real-time measurement, Jarrett focuses on lowest preventable mortality with an emphasis on best practices to head off hospital-acquired conditions such as central line infections, surgical site infections, pressure ulcers, falls with injuries, sepsis, etc. While Jarrett studies data for the entire Northwell system, he also drills down closer to the front lines of care by accessing and acting upon dashboards at the unit level "so that every nursing unit will know how they are doing. It is important because it is really the front-line troops that are the ones that really make the change. Leaders can get people motivated but true performance improvement comes from front line people saying, 'this is the way it works. This is what we have got to do.' We have a lot of system-level stuff and hospital-level stuff and now we are bringing it down to unit level." Jarrett says that sharing comparative data with various hospitals and clinics can spur improvement. Every month at a meeting of medical directors from the 21 hospitals, Jarrett displays a slide with the latest infection rates for each facility. "Having that data out there pulls everybody up a little bit," he says, "because they do not want to be the one that had four of these infections last month when everybody else had only one last month. It motivates them to push a little harder."

"You give them data that is wrong and they blow you out of the water."

Typically, quality relates to clinical outcomes, but in an age when the cost of care is so steep Jarrett believes that it is necessary to include the concept of value within the quality equation. Value, in one sense, means eliminating unneeded care—"when we do things we do not need to do which increase risk for the patient" and drive up costs. Unnecessary care or overuse is in many respects the bane of the U.S. health care system. Research indicates that anywhere from 15 to 30 percent of the dollars spent on care in the U.S. are wasted on unnecessary procedures, tests, appointments, surgeries, etc. This is due to administrative inefficiency and physicians' preferences, derived from their training, for how best to care for patients. Changing the way doctors do certain things is difficult. *You mean to tell me I have been doing it wrong all these years!?* "There is the difficulty of abandoning things that you learned a long time ago that seemed to work but now the data says that you should change and abandon what you are doing," observes Dr. Lawrence Smith. "Do it a different way because the outcomes are better. That is a psychic struggle that many physicians have difficulty with. What you were doing was not wrong. It is just that now there is evidence that there is a better way to do it. I think that getting people to understand that collecting data about their own outcomes is not about gotcha. It is about continuous improvement. The data is not a personal assault for which you should have an emotional reaction. It is simply information to allow you to continuously get better. As care delivery evolves new research indicates that, for example, there is no clinical evidence to support testing for prostate cancer in low-risk patients over age 70. To get physicians to change is only possible through the use of good data; data indicating that perhaps there may be a better way than the way they having been trained and doing something for years or even decades."

"It's really about education and showing them the data," says Jarrett. "With bundled payments for joint replacements, for example, the biggest element of value difference or cost difference among different physicians is not the cost of the prosthesis because a lot of that has been standardized. And almost all patients stay in the hospital the same number of days so the difference in cost is really around the issue of whether they go home from the hospital or whether they go to some other facility for rehab. A small number of people need to go to rehab but the great majority do not. They should be going directly home." Yet going home, rather than to a reha-bilitation facility, is perceived by some patients as skipping an important step; depriving them of care to which they are entitled. "But we can provide the necessary rehab at home as an outpatient and we can make you just as well and give you just as much rehab as you need at much lower cost," says Dr. David Battinelli. In fact, he says, as outpatients, patients can typically get more rehab work for lower cost than if they are confined to a rehab facility.

Some doctors do very well getting their patients directly home after surgery. Some do less well. "We have one doctor at Lenox Hill Hospital who has a five percent rate of sending people to rehab while there is a surgeon at another facility and 30 percent of his patients are going to rehab instead of going directly home," says Jarrett. "The patients are the same age group, the same conditions, everything is comparable and you show the data and that gets their attention." The idea is not to embarrass doctors, but when a physician sees that he or she lags well behind on an important measure, they tend to act quickly. *What is a better way? What are these other surgeons doing that I am not?* In this case, the surgeon with the higher rate of sending patients to rehab can focus on appropriate physical therapy before surgery and greater emphasis on follow-up physical therapy. "They respond to data as long as it is accurate data," says Jarrett. "You cannot give them data that is wrong. You give them data that is wrong and they blow you out of the water. You lose six months." In the new value-based payment world physicians have a growing awareness that providing high quality care at a reasonable cost is more important than ever. Says Jarrett: "Doctors are beginning to realize that if they are inefficient in order to produce good quality data, they are going to be excluded from contracts."

Burnout

No one argues that quality measurement, from Press Ganey or the real-time data Jarrett identifies, is anything but positive for patients, but there is another side to the data/transparency coin and it is about pressure on doctors. The pursuit of measurement takes its toll on physicians. A number of the trends in health care in the past decade or so, in fact, have conspired to pressure doctors to the point where burnout among physicians has become "a huge deal," says Dr. Lawrence Smith. Dr. David Blumenthal and David Squires from the Commonwealth Fund observed[5] that some studies suggest that "American physicians are severely stressed and unhappy" and asking a key question: "Why should we worry about unhappy doctors?" Blumenthal and Squires, citing an article by Lawrence P. Casalino of Weill Cornell Medical College and Francis J. Crosson of the American Medical Association, suggest that "reduced well-being and satisfaction could theoretically undermine their diligence, cognitive functioning, and relationships with patients. These effects could reduce the quality of physicians' decisions and patients' adherence to physician recommendations."

Measurement is only one factor contributing to burnout. Electronic Medical Records are powerful tools, but, to many physicians, these machines feel like a ball and chain constraining their freedom and impeding their productivity. And surely there is something tyrannical about the EMR. Doctors enter the exam room and find themselves facing the screen as they type rather than facing the patient as they listen. In medical practices where a new Electronic Health Record is installed, one with which doctors are unfamiliar, the break-in period can be riddled with angst. In a broad survey of Northwell physicians in late 2016, the Electronic Medical Record was cited by a large number of doctors as a source of frustration, according to Dr. Nash. Doctors complain that 10 hours seeing patients generates additional hours of documentation on a computer during breaks as well as nights and weekends. That this is in line with results at other large health systems does not comfort Nash. "We are exploring a number of ways to lessen that 'pain point' through enhanced functionality, expanded training and support, and exploration of a variety of different 'scribing' strategies"—having support staff members engage with the EMR while the physician focuses on the patient. The goal, he says, is "to help diminish the burden of interaction with the systems."

In addition to measurement and electronic health records, Conigliaro says the sheer volume of work contributes to burn-out. "We're asked to see more and more and sicker patients," he says. "The fact that we can do more and take care of more means we have to. Back in the day, there were some conditions for which we had no effective treatments. Now I have more things that I can treat, which means more work."

There are other complications from burnout. Dr. Jarrett notes that dissatisfaction among physicians causes some of the most experienced doctors to retire early even as Baby Boomers reach retirement age and require more care than ever. "Baby Boomers are hitting 65 and older and this will go on for another 18 years or so, yet the people taking care of them are millennials who have a different view of work–life balance," he says. "How will this play out in terms of delivery of care?" Physician dissatisfaction is also the best predictor of early retirement and reduced work hours, which could exacerbate a predicted physician shortage, especially in primary care. Some experts are suggesting that the well-being of the health care workforce is important enough to be added to the Triple Aim as a fourth central goal of health policy: better health, better care, lower costs, and now, joy in work.

"The night you are not *on call, you ought to be able to get to your kid's birthday party."*

The pace of change in health care stresses doctors. "They need to work harder and harder when you are measured by productivity," says Dr. Smith. "Burnout results from overwork, hyper-responsibility, the inability to openly admit and mourn your mistakes when they hurt people. Burnout is found in many professions to a small degree and overwhelmingly in caregiver professions where you are responsible for another person. When you are responsible there is a lot of burden to walk around with and nobody gets it right all of the time." The financial squeeze in health care is a factor as well as doctors try to "respond to the economics of care while feeling that they have maintained

their integrity in terms of quality of care," says Smith. He inter-
prets part of the issue with physician burnout as attributable to
"this kind of fall from privilege that a lot of physicians feel. That
being a doctor feels different and is different today than it was
certainly when I went to medical school in the 1970s."

Smith, Nash, and other physician leaders have found a
number of strategies to try and combat burnout within the
organization. "One approach is camaraderie and a place to
moan and groan," says Smith. "It is private. Physicians need
time in the doctor's cafeteria where they can scream and yell
about patients and what they do to them, and the nursing
staff, and the hospital administration. '*This damn value based
bullshit. The EMR that does not work and just slowed them
down to a grinding halt.*' I think you need a place with trusted
people who you know have empathy for the same situation
where you can ventilate."

As much or more than anything else, some sense of control
over work–life balance can make a difference. "There is a lot
of evidence that when you feel the least in control of your situation at work, it accentuates the likelihood you will burnout,"
says Smith. "I think you have to think about that is a possible
reason why interns and residents burnout. Because they have
such low control and inordinate work hours. That combination
is really deadly. Little things like work life balance is anathema
to most physicians because it is not possible in many situations. But we have to recognize people need to have balance.
We get it. The night you are on call for your ten other doctors in your group, you do not have a balance that night so
get it together. You are not going to the Knicks game while
being on call for ten other doctors, not unless you like standing out on the street with your cell phone the whole time. On
the other hand the night you are *not* on call, you ought to be
able to get to your kid's birthday party. It is not acceptable
if you cannot do that. I think when you start to create a culture where it is okay for those things and where doctors work
together and recognize that they are covering for their friend,

but to be able to really be free of that burden when the other things in your life need to get done. Having some control over schedule is important."

Teamwork helps mitigate some burnout. Primary care doctors may see as many as one hundred patients in a work week. Multiply that number of visits times blood tests, prescriptions (sometimes a half dozen or more medications per patient), follow-up instructions, referrals to specialists and imaging tests, and it adds up to an amount of work that no individual, however brilliant, can keep track of alone. "A lot of medical students," says Conigliaro, "look at primary care as, basically, 'I am alone. I have to take care of all this stuff on a patient.' At the same time, primary care physicians are paid less than specialists in other fields and quite often primary care doctors have only minimal control over what happens to their patients." That old model bears little resemblance to what Conigliaro, Pilapil, and their colleagues are doing with team-based care. "We are saying, 'it's not like that. You have a core group of patients that you take care of and you run a team that takes care of them'. Making sure everybody on the team kind of works to their fullest decreases burnout."

Endnotes

1. How High-Need patients Experience Health Care in the United States; findings from the 2016 Commonwealth Fund Survey of High-Need Patients; Analysis of the 2016 Commonwealth Fund Survey of High-Need Patients, June–September 2016.
2. The study also found that "adults with high medical needs often have unmet emotional and social needs. The survey results indicate that this group is more likely than the general population to report experiencing emotional distress that was difficult to cope with on their own in the past two years. Nearly four of 10 (37%) high-need respondents reported often feeling socially isolated, including lacking companionship, feeling left out, or feeling lonely or isolated from others, compared

with 15 percent of other adults (Exhibit 1). Almost two-thirds (62%) of high-need respondents report stress or worry about material hardships, such as being unable to pay for housing, utilities, or nutritious meals, compared to only one-third of other adults (32%). Furthermore, six of 10 (59%) high-need adults report being somewhat or very concerned about being a burden to family or friends …"

3. Patient-centered medical home is intended to fix that and Northwell instituted its first NCQA-designated patient centered medical home in 2008.

4. The program ("Screening, brief intervention and referral to treatment") he applies has proven so effective that it has been adopted by New York State health officials as a standard that should be used with all patients.

5. [Physician dissatisfaction: Diagnosis and Treatment; CMWF Tuesday, December 13, 2016; By David Blumenthal, M.D. and David Squires]

Chapter 7

Rory

*"We have become comfortable admitting that we don't
know what we are doing. I am a doctor. We just do
not do that. But the ability to do it is now embedded
within the learning culture where people have become
self-aware and self-critical and then self-correcting."*

Dr. Marty Doerfler

"I got the ball!"

The basketball bounced to the side and as it skittered
across the school gym, Rory Staunton, a 12-year-old bundle of
energy and joy, dove for it, scraping his elbow as he did so.
That night Rory told his mother that he had fallen and that the
gym teacher had bandaged his arm, but, most importantly, he
told her: *"I got the ball!"*[1] The next day Rory was quite sick
with a fever and vomiting. His mom took him to his pediatrician. A flu bug was going around they said and sent him to
the emergency room to treat him for dehydration. An ER doctor checked him out and accepted the pediatrician's conclusion. The ER team gave him two bags of fluids intravenously
as well as an anti-nausea drug. After the fluids, a doctor
checked him again, said he seemed better, and sent him home
with instructions to take Tylenol. During the night, Rory got

sicker, his fever climbing to 104. As his condition worsened, Rory's parents took him back to the New York University Langone Medical Center emergency room. He was examined again and admitted to the hospital, but it was too late. Two days later, Ciaran and Orlaith Staunton lost their precious son.

"Nobody knew what sepsis was."

Rory's death was caused by sepsis, which kills more people in the United States every year than cancers of the breast and colon combined. Sepsis occurs when the body's attempt to fight infection triggers systemic inflammation that can gravely damage lungs, kidneys, and heart. There is something particularly malevolent about sepsis. It often shows little of itself, not unlike an iceberg where most of what is happening is unseen except to the careful observer. It is frequently misidentified as other simpler ailments requiring minimal treatment, just as happened in Rory's case. The chills, fever, and rapid heart rate which indicate possible sepsis are also indicators of numerous other conditions and this is what makes sepsis so treacherous, for it routinely lulls patients, family members, and medical professionals into a sense of complacency. Sepsis hides under the camouflage of seemingly harmless symptoms, secreting itself within the body, wrecking silent havoc until discovered, often too late.

By no means is it a new disease. In fact, it is ancient. Originally, the word sepsis was used by Hippocrates around 400 BC "and is derived from the Greek word *sipsi (make rotten)*."[2] Dr. Martin E. Doerfler recalls a sepsis expert doing grand rounds at Northwell and reading from a thousand year old document "describing this condition of fever and infection as one that is difficult to grasp and get your arms around until it is easy to grasp and get your arms around because the patient is dying of it. When it is easy to treat it is hard to diagnose and when it is easy to find it is hard to treat."

Michael Dowling became aware of the fact that sepsis was the largest single contributor to mortality at Northwell Health and that "we had a significantly higher mortality for sepsis [as indicated on Healthgrades] than we are expected to have," says Doerfler. As Dowling drilled down on the issue he realized the staggering global scope of the sepsis problem and he decided to act on both a global and local scale. Globally, Dowling convened the Merinoff Symposium in the Fall of 2010 at the Feinstein Institute of Medical Research at Northwell which attracted many of the world's leading sepsis experts from eighteen different nations. Dr. Kevin Tracey, a neurosurgeon who heads the Feinstein Institute, had spent years researching sepsis and had written an important book on the subject (*Fatal Sequence: The Killer Within*).

"We decided to have a meeting here, to call out the problem of sepsis," recalls Tracey. "One of the big problems with sepsis, we realized, was that although it was the leading cause of death in hospitalized patients in the United States, nobody outside medicine knew what it was. You could ask your mother, father, your friends, or their friends, but nobody knew what sepsis was." Thus, was held the first meeting of the Global Sepsis Alliance with the goal to create a "public definition"[3] of sepsis, a "molecular definition"[4] of sepsis, and to sound a "global call to action to recognize sepsis as a medical emergency." The scope of the sepsis problem is so vast that the Global Sepsis Alliance includes nearly 500,000 medical experts from around the world. In writing about the new initiative that emerged from the Merinoff Symposium, Christopher J. Czura, PhD, from the Feinstein Institute, compared the sepsis challenge to the threat posed by polio more than six decades earlier. "In the first half of the twentieth century," he wrote, "the polio pandemic spread across much of the world, afflicting hundreds of thousands each year … [and] a diverse group from many industries, both public and private, collaborated to develop a comprehensible message that defined the problem of polio, described its prevalence and mortality, and communicated the barriers to diagnosing and treating it effectively." Five decades later polio has been all but eradicated. Would that be possible with sepsis? Or was sepsis so challenging and complex that it would elude even the most robust efforts for years to come? At Northwell, Mark Solazzo went so far as to declare sepsis as the number one clinical priority of the health system and during the Merinoff gathering Dowling promised that Northwell would reduce the mortality rate from sepsis by fifty percent in five years. "And scientists are there," recalls Tracey "and they hear this and they're thinking—*'that's what he thinks. Listen to the layman. He doesn't understand'*."

One of the things that drives Dowling's continuing determination on sepsis is that he had met with Rory's parents. Like Dowling, the Stauntons had come from Ireland and settled in New York. He felt a natural kinship with them and the power of their grief and of their determination to see what could be done to protect other children, was deeply affecting. When Dowling and others from Northwell met with the Stauntons, as they did on a number of occasions, the only solace they could offer them was that they would do everything in their power to gain a deeper understanding of sepsis and to try and figure out a treatment approach to save lives.

"Just shoot me."

But the truth was that, early on, the Northwell sepsis work wasn't going as planned. A task force of doctors and nurses had been charged with improving sepsis care but the group was stuck. Dr. John D'Angelo, an emergency room physician, found the initial meetings of the group more discouraging than anything. A major part of the problem was that critical care physicians and emergency room doctors viewed sepsis from radically different perspectives. In the task force, critical care doctors focused on septic shock in the ICU rather than on the challenge of identifying and treating sepsis at an earlier stage, such as in the Emergency Room where D'Angelo and his colleagues encountered it. These were entirely different problems with widely varying symptoms and solutions. If the task force couldn't agree on where the problem lay, how could it make any progress?

In an effort to break the logjam Dr. Kenneth Abrams, the Associate Chief Medical Officer, decided to reorganize the task force under a new leader and he thought Doerfler was the right candidate. Doerfler joined the system in 2010 to focus on spreading the notion of reliable evidence-based practice throughout Northwell. In previous positions both at medical centers and in private industry, Doerfler had demonstrated an ability to lead change. He understood the science and theory behind many different concepts, including evidence-based medicine, but he also demonstrated a nuts and bolts ability to get things done on the front lines. Doerfler had trained in internal medicine at Bellevue and NYU before heading to the National Institutes of Health for five years to focus on hard science related to sepsis. He returned to NYU as Chief of Critical Care for the Department of Medicine while also setting up a laboratory to deepen his research in and supervise clinical trials on sepsis drugs. But it was outside the lab that he proved most effective. "I was pulled into administrative and clinical areas," he says. "Very importantly, early in my tenure at NYU, I recognized that as someone with authority to determine the rules of the game, I could actually impact care more than when I was a physician with my own hands." After NYU, Doerfler joined a company called VISICU in its earliest days and played a key role in the company's applications related to critical care telemedicine. It proved to be the first commercially successful telehealth company in the world.

Doerfler arrived at Northwell ready to take on the role of leading clinical change. Barely a month after he started, however, Dr. Abrams, Doerfler's boss, stopped him in the hall. "'I need you to take on something'," Doerfler recalls Abrams telling him. Abrams said that the sepsis work Dowling had kicked off in 2009 was not accelerating as quickly as clinical leaders wanted. "Ken said to me: 'I need you to take this on'." Doerfler was an expert in sepsis. He knew it from a clinical perspective and from a research perspective but coming to Northwell he thought he had put sepsis behind him for the truth was that, through the years he had come to believe that maybe sepsis wasn't a solvable problem. "It is a *really* big problem, plus, it had been a piece of my career literally decades ago and I was over and done with it." After his meeting with Abrams, Doerfler was deflated—this was *not* how he had expected to start his new career at Northwell.

"I went home and looked in the mirror and said, 'Just shoot me'."

"It would be like telling the French that they needed to eat Chinese food all the time."

Doerfler was well aware of the clinical conflict around sepsis. Most of the academic research done on the subject had focused on ICU patients for the simple reason that people gravely ill with sepsis are moved into an ICU and that is where they die. Nearly all initiatives related to sepsis—including the international collaboration known as the Surviving Sepsis campaign—had come predominantly from doctors focused on critical care. "For the past two decades the focus on sepsis has been in the critical care community," says Doerfler. "Yet we saw that the opportunity begins in the Emergency Department. So in essence we had an intellectual conflict between two groups who see the world differently. Our critical care people were arguing over the last three inches of the journey, arguing over the fine points of what you do at the extreme end of the patient's condition not about the basics."

The task force within Northwell had been operating for a about a year prior to Doerfler's arrival on the scene and the division was so sharp that some leaders within the emergency medicine group, who felt their voices were not being heard, chose not to participate. These doctors knew that the reality was that many patients presented in emergency rooms with infections having the potential to trigger an overwhelming immune reaction and inflame vital organs—long before patients experienced the septic shock characterized by the failure of respiratory, cardiac and other system failures in the body. Broadening the conversation to include early stage sepsis symptoms was contrary to the default thinking about sepsis as shock. "This was a major barrier," recalls Darlene Parmentier, an emergency room nurse manager with expertise in sepsis. "The team couldn't get people out of the septic shock world."

That is not to say that no progress was made early on. While D'Angelo felt that the first three or four task force meetings were largely unproductive, he took matters into his own hands at a certain point and drafted what would later become the system's first sepsis screening tool. He presented an algorithm and in-patient order set at a June 2009 system quality meeting. "We started creating a database to collect the baseline data against which we would track progress," says D'Angelo.

Doerfler had expertise in critical care but in this case he believed that the emergency department physicians were correct—that the focus of the discussions needed to change. "It was clear that the greatest opportunity was to move upstream to patients at an earlier stage of their illness or at least at an earlier stage of their presentation to the hospital," he says. Thus, one of the first steps was to reset and to gain a better understanding of how sepsis could be dealt with in the emergency room. Applying treatment criteria from a critical care ICU in the emergency department would not work. "They are different environments," says Doerfler. "It would be like telling the French that they needed to eat Chinese food all the time."

When they joined forces in July 2010, Doerfler and D'Angelo were thinking along similar lines. Doerfler notes that D'Angelo played a crucial role. His active participation on the task force signaled to other emergency department physicians throughout the system that they had a strong voice in the ongoing discussions. To round out the leadership of the task force, Doerfler and D'Angelo asked Darlene Parmentier, to join them. "John and I asked Darlene to join us because we thought that nursing was a critical part of the needed leadership," says Doerfler. "One of the things that he and I both have as a consistent element to how we work is that we have a very high level of respect for the role of nursing in all of this." Nurses in the emergency room are the first caregivers to see patients and, in many instances, nurses are able to detect possible indicators of sepsis before a physician has even examined the patient. Doerfler, D'Angelo, and Parmentier identified about a dozen clinical leaders across disciplines—emergency and critical care physicians, nurse leaders, and quality officers—and brought them together. They began to refocus from the narrow view of sepsis as shock to a broader view. "We want to focus on the spectrum," says D'Angelo, "not just on people already in trouble on the extreme end of the spectrum. We want to identify it as early as possible and most of that identification and early intervention is going to occur in emergency departments." But this was a Rubik's Cube in the dark. How could you tell which patients arriving in the ER were at risk for sepsis? In the ICU it was simpler: Patients were in advanced septic shock. But in the ER a patient arriving with a fever and respiratory difficulty may or may not have sepsis. Thus, there were two difficult questions: First, how do you *identify* it? And, second, how do you *treat* it?

"When you looked at the data, if you looked nationally in published literature, a third of the patients who are discharged with the diagnosis of sepsis were recognized in the emergency department," says Doerfler. "Another third had it in the emergency department, but were not recognized until they were in the hospital. And another third had developed it in the hospital. So two thirds of all sepsis naturally walks in your front door. In this health system, it is 80-plus percent. So if you are going to deal with this, you deal with it in the emergency room."

One of the reasons sepsis is such a big, complicated problem in the U.S. and throughout the world, says Doerfler, "is that any patient with a significant bacterial infection [could have sepsis] and it is very hard to detect the transition from pneumonia, for example, to pneumonia with inflammatory response injuring the body—a significant sepsis episode. It's all silent, hidden, and you don't feel any pain when there is damage being done to your lungs and kidneys. With sepsis, not severe sepsis and shock, you have a fever, you have an infection and your heart rate is up a little bit. You may have a mildly elevated white count. You have sepsis." The strict definition of sepsis, in other words, would corral many more patients than were actually in danger. "A lot of people present to the ED with strep throat or other less severe infections and have a pulse over 90, temperature of 101 or greater and would fit the" standard criteria for diagnosing sepsis known as Systemic Inflammatory Response Syndrome (SIRS), says D'Angelo. A 22-year-old college kid, for example, with a severe sore throat, fever, and mildly elevated heart rate has the elements required to meet sepsis according to SIRS guidelines. "But you can't apply those rules to everyone," says Doerfler. "That kid, who looks fine and is being given ibuprofen and oral antibiotics and sent home, could have been sent to the intensive care unit under the traditional guidelines. So you cannot hold an ED physician accountable for these metrics that have been developed by critical care people to say here is how you care for septic shock. So you had this real split that was based upon two different realities."

Task force members had lively discussions, going back and forth debating definitional details. Compromise and consensus were important. Team members all agreed, of course, that a patient with a heart rate of 150 beats per minute was very sick, says Doerfler, "so in the meeting we marched that down and everyone agreed at 120 but we when we went below that some people didn't agree so we said, 'okay, sold at 120.' We did the same thing on respiratory, 'sold at 24 [breaths per minute].' Blood pressure was already there [at <90]. We added in altered mental status. Someone who comes in confused meets the criteria. 'Yes, sold,' everyone agreed on these criteria which gave us a consensus base set of terms to start applying every day in the ED."

The four criteria; nicknamed super SIRS, were:

- Pulse >120
- Blood pressure <90 systolic
- Respiratory rate >24
- Altered mental status

The presence of these elements did not indicate for certain that a patient had sepsis, but they did make clear that the patient was quite sick and needed immediate attention from a doctor. Reaching this definition "was huge," says D'Angelo, "because now we had defined, objective triage criteria that our triage nurses could use to escalate a case to their ED team. Such escalation later became hardwired across the network via a 'Code Sepsis' which, like in heart attack (Code STEMI) and stroke (Code Neuro), conditioned ED providers to responding with a similar sense of urgency. We led everyone to see early sepsis and, more importantly, patients at risk for severe sepsis, as a true emergency and, just like time is muscle in a heart attack and time is brain in a stroke, rapid evaluation and treatment was critical and could have a dramatic impact on the patients outcome."

Four Life-Saving Steps

With a definition in place, the task force members turned their attention to defining the treatment for patients meeting the super SIRS criteria. This was an area rich with material. Physicians throughout the world had determined that the most effective intervention involved a series of steps over a period of six to twelve hours. Doerfler, D'Angelo, Parmentier and their colleagues decided to focus on the four critical steps that should be taken in the first three hours:

- Draw blood cultures before giving antibiotics.
- Administer aggressive antibiotics. Must be started within 180 minutes for all sepsis patients and within 60 minutes for patients with possible severe sepsis (i.e., met "Super Sirs" Criteria).
- Serum lactate test to determine whether patient has severe sepsis including organ dysfunction.
- Any evidence of organ dysfunction requires early aggressive fluids. Sepsis with organ dysfunction (Severe Sepsis) has a far higher rate of mortality.

The task force had made progress. They had defined criteria for identifying early signs of sepsis and they had agreed on a precise approach to treatment. At this point, you could step back and say, *well done*. This was important work, no doubt. But the reality was that the most difficult part of the job lay ahead—for now the challenge was to take the definition and treatment and spread it throughout all 21 Northwell hospitals and embedding it so permanently in the culture that it would be sustained 24 hours a day 365 days a year for every patient. And doing so involved identifying countless small steps toward improvement. "It's about focus," says Mark Solazzo, "on small cycles of change. Sepsis care isn't about taking leaps forward, it is about focus and reliably doing many small things." On paper, these are simple steps, but the clinical reality is more complex. "In order to get antibiotics into a patient within three hours," says Doerfler, "I first need to get the patient from the front door into the room, get their clothes off, get vital signs, establish an IV, recognize they have an infection, get a doctor in to confirm, get blood and lactate tests sent to the lab, get an order written for the right antibiotics based upon the test results, have that order get to the pharmacy, the pharmacy makes up the drug, the drug gets to the patient, the nurse hangs it." There were barriers everywhere. The lactate test, for example, required not just sending it out to the lab, but making sure the results got back to the doctor in a timely way and this meant working with lab and transport personnel to make sure they understood the importance of a rapid response. The work required collaborating for improved focus and response times not only with the lab but with a variety of other departments.

"It was a major fundamental shift."

And here was yet another challenge: How would you measure performance? In other words, how would you know whether a particular team at a particular hospital was applying the definition appropriately and delivering treatment in a timely and consistent fashion? How would the team know whether they were improving? Certainly reducing overall mortality from sepsis was the goal, but intermediate process measures were needed to make sure the teams in all hospitals were taking the steps needed to protect patients. Of all the steps in the process getting antibiotics started in patients was the most important. The task force members decided to focus on that as a key measure—to calculate the percentage of cases in which clinicians were able to get antibiotics into patients within 180 minutes. "We needed to have reliable information," says Doerfler. "You get physicians and nurses into a room and you tell them you are underperforming on something and if they can realistically tell you that your data is wrong, you have no credibility. Even if you do have some credibility, they are not going to listen when you say, 'I want to be at 70 percent,' and they say, 'by my data say I am already at 80 percent so we are done, right?'" The task force members reviewed the literature, studied recommendations for treatment and measurement from various other sources and reached consensus on what was best for their patients.

"One of the important things that I have learned is that measurement for regulatory compliance, the things that we are held accountable by government agencies, are not the same as measurements for improvement," says Doerfler. "We got folks together and we talked about improvement. We said, 'okay what number would actually indicate that we are doing a good job?' So we worked on that. One of the concerns for the emergency department was around the concept of *time zero*. When does the clock start on for measurement? What is the point at which you hold someone accountable for having gotten something done within a certain period of time?" The literature was based upon the clock starting when the patient arrives in the emergency room, but the ED physicians would have none of that. *How can you hold me accountable,* they said, *for what happens in the half an hour before I even see the patient?*

So the question, in a fairly tense discussion, was: What is a reasonable measurement standard for improvement? What should time zero be? And the answer after a back and forth discussion, was twofold. The measurement clock would start at the time a patient met Super SIRS criteria, which could be upon arrival at the emergency department or hours later. Or time zero was when the doctor first examined the patient and suspected sepsis (as opposed to a lesser serious infection such as strep) and ordered the sepsis blood work. From that point, the doctor would have 180 minutes to send blood cultures, begin administering antibiotics, get the results back for a lactate test, and administer IV fluids aggressively even if lab results, which served as evidence of organ injury, had not yet returned.

"Gaining agreement on time zero was a crucial moment in moving the work forward," says Doerfler. "It broke down a major barrier that ED clinicians had reasonably erected. When we had agreement, the ED clinicians were immediately comfortable being held accountable and resistance stopped. It was clear that we would not measure them on things they did not control. It was a major fundamental shift." Another step forward came when Dr. Bruce Hirsh, an experienced infectious disease physician, told the task force members that, as Doerfler recalls it, "'folks, we have to agree to agree. We are going to come up with something and once we settle on it then we are going to go out of the room and move forward'.

There were many issues and anything that we didn't agree on went off the table and we said, 'okay, we will get to that later.' Once we agreed to agree, we moved fairly quickly."

In difficult work such as this, few things are more important in the process of change management than making clear to frontline workers that you are on their side. If doctors and nurses believe that you are setting standards that are essentially punitive, they will resist. If, however, you trust that the people at the front lines who do the work know the work, then doctors and nurses will believe that you are there to help them improve care. This is the kind of environment in which concurrent review and small measurements—*did we get the lactate to the lab in a timely way on Thursday?*—are possible. These are the measures that help answer the crucial underlying question in all improvement work: *Are we doing what we think we are doing?* If the measures you are tracking actually are indicators of improvement, then clinicians get on board. Because Doerfler, D'Angelo, and Parmentier worked with the front line teams to define what metrics they would follow, clinicians were comfortable. "The data was going to be accurate enough to tell us we were getting better or worse and because of that people believed in it," says Doerfler. "For our lactate measure for example, we had agreed on not simply getting a lactate ordered within three hours. We wanted it back to the doctor and the results in the doctor's hands within 90 minutes. That was part of the consensus. You get those things done; first the clinicians feel like you are listening to them and not just whipping them to get something done quicker. Now, the entire organization begins to feel like we can change and we can change around a purpose and we can prove that that change was or wasn't worthwhile, because you don't just want to change for the sake of change."

"*I do not need help. We know what we are doing.*"

During the course of his time at Northwell, Michael Dowling had come to know a number of the leaders at the Institute for

Healthcare Improvement (IHI) in Cambridge, Massachusetts. The institute was founded in the early 1990s by Dr. Donald Berwick and a small group of colleagues who believed that there was the potential to make significant improvements in the overall quality and safety of health care in the United States. Berwick, in fact, was a central figure in the Institute of Medicine reports *To Err Is Human* (1999) and *Crossing the Quality Chasm (2001)*. The expertise of the IHI team was targeting clinical problems such as sepsis, scouring the country for the best practices, and then helping to spread those practices to other locations. IHI teams had identified how-to guidelines for preventing central-line associated bloodstream infections, ventilator-associated pneumonia, and other such ailments that were all-too common in U.S. hospitals but that were highly preventable with consistent application of best practices. IHI CEO Maureen Bisognano had participated in the Merinoff sessions and she and her teams within IHI were among the international leaders in the Surviving Sepsis campaign. Dowling thought IHI could help Northwell improve its performance on sepsis as well as in other areas and he also wanted Northwell teams to learn improvement science from IHI.

When Doerfler was informed that IHI personnel would be coming in to Northwell to work on the sepsis, however, he was none too pleased. "I remember very specifically feeling that we didn't need IHI for the sepsis work," he recalls. "I was annoyed because I had expertise in all of this and my reaction was *I do not need help. We know what we are doing. Leave us alone.* We had made real progress. I considered my own skills to be significant in the change management space. Northwell had a team of improvement science personnel who are experts in Six Sigma and LEAN methodologies. I had spent a decade working on physician behavior change in the telehealth arena prior to coming here. I did not see that they were going to add real value and I felt we would lose credit for everything we just did that we had been working on." This kind of response is not altogether unusual when IHI arrives to work at an organization, but, fairly soon after IHI began working with Northwell at the end of 2011/beginning of 2012, it became clear that the IHI team possessed meaningful experience in how to spread improvements throughout a large system. Importantly, when the IHI team arrived they also brought with them physicians from other health systems who had confronted exactly the kinds of challenges Doerfler and his team were facing. "They came in and they brought their methodology and some outside experts and helped us create a model for improvement and it made a difference," says Doerfler. "They come in and first they listened to what we had done and where we were and did not come in and say 'we have a formula you need to stick with it and change what you have done.' They actually appreciated what we did but they brought some tools into the discussion. I learned a lot."

Among the tools in the IHI box was something called a "driver diagram," a process which begins with simple questions: "What are you trying to accomplish? How will you know a change is an improvement? What changes can you make that will result in an improvement?" Often referred to as a "key" driver diagram, this "is a simple, visual tool that will assist you to systematically plan and structure your improvement project. It will help you understand the logic of your project and where you are going with your improvement initiative. It is a living document that can be updated at every team meeting where drivers and change concepts can be discussed and agreed upon … A driver diagram will also help to define which aspects of the system should be measured and monitored to see if the changes and interventions are effective, and if the underlying causal theories are correct."[5]

Doerfler, D'Angelo, and Parmentier found the driver diagram exercise to be clarifying. Doerfler offers a simple analogy. "Let's say you want to lose weight—that's your outcome. Your primary driver is *I can exercise more and I can eat less.* So, look at how you can exercise more. *I can run, I can walk, I can swim.* Go back to swimming: *If I get up an hour earlier*

*and drive 30 minutes to the pool, no that won't work because
I only have 10 minutes to swim, I am not going to accomplish
anything. If I get up an hour earlier and I have the exer-cycle
in the basement that I don't use and I use that for 30 minutes.
Okay I am going to try that."*

The focus on basics helped the team figure out how to
get antibiotics to patients more rapidly by narrowing down
the type of antibiotics most often used with sepsis patients.
What if you had a small number of key drugs readily available within the emergency department for rapid use instead
of having to go to the pharmacy every time antibiotics are
needed and go through the whole request process? By making that one small change, the team took 20 minutes out of
the process thus accelerating infusion of antibiotics to patients
which, in turn, reduces mortality. "We worked on a lot of little
pieces," says Doerfler. "How long does it take you to get a
patient from coming in the door to getting a central temperature? How can we work to cut a few minutes off of that? If we
cut a few minutes off of every step, it adds up and we continue to do that work."

The key to those efforts was asking frontline teams to
participate in the project and all its elements. Frontline workers know where the slowdowns are and where the opportunities for improvement are. "The folks at Northwell were
already very capable improvers," says Andrea Kabcenell, a
vice president at IHI. "In our work together we found that the
work in the ED is essentially a reliability problem. Doing the
things reliably that they know need to be done. And they had
a superb use of measurement. They would add some measurement at the front line and then ask, 'okay, on Thursday
we measured this, did we get it right all day Thursday? Let's
see how we can get better on Friday.'" IHI established a
collaborative learning opportunity for a number of organizations throughout the country working on sepsis and regular
calls with the participants allowed the sharing of ideas and
questions.

"Part of the IHI methodology was to conduct quarterly learning sessions at which the teams from each hospital tasked with leading the effort at their facility would gather," says D'Angelo. "Usually these were teams of six to eight people including an Emergency Department physician and nurse, an inpatient nurse, and maybe a hospitalist, and someone from the quality department. At these sessions participants would learn about improvement science methodology-driver diagrams, process maps, goal setting, how to use their data in a meaningful way, how to conduct test of change, etc. We would also hear clinical talks specific to sepsis from internal experts as well as from the sepsis experts IHI brought to the table."

In between learning sessions the teams met to work on their site specific sepsis goals and initiatives. At each learning session the teams were tasked with providing the larger group (all learning session participants) with a 10–15 minute presentation on their efforts the prior three months (goals, results, barriers, challenges, next steps, etc.). The larger group would then provide feedback. "Initially this was intimidating to the teams," says D'Angelo. "There was fear of 'looking bad,' and hesitation in sharing their data and struggles. But by the third learning session the culture shifted dramatically and teams were sharing successes and failures, what was working and what was not. It was important also that the audience members—meaning the peers of those presenting—were quick to share that they had had similar challenges and they would share any solutions they might have come up with. This not only occurred at the quarterly learning sessions with an IHI team on site, but it also started to happen in the weekly sepsis conference calls and at the monthly Northwell system sepsis task force meetings. This is when we really started to see improvement and the determination and engagement of the teams was contagious and amazing to watch. At one of these meetings a team reported that they were facing a real challenge delivering the IV fluid as quickly as required because of a limitation in the new IV pumps that were rolled out across the organization. Once that comment was made you could see the heads nodding in agreement around the room. Darlene then stood up and reported they had experienced the same thing so they played with solutions and ultimately learned that they could place two of these pumps on a single IV pole and use tubing that would merge the output from each and deliver the desired amount of fluid in the desired time through a single large bore IV catheter inserted into the patient. This then quickly spread and became a standard part of the 'Code Sepsis' process at all sites."

The partnership with IHI helped accelerate the improvement work throughout the system. Doerfler, D'Angelo, Parmentier, and their colleagues along with the IHI team listened to what the frontline doctors and nurses were telling them what was delaying the administration of antibiotics, what was slowing down the lactate tests, what was preventing the lab from getting blood work back as fast as it needed to be back. "In the IHI methodology and LEAN methodology, the true experts are the people who do the work," says Doerfler. This is where the improvement science came in and the heart of that was to test various small improvements. To do this the teams implemented a PDSA approach. These Plan–Do–Study–Act tests of change are simple to do and helped quickly determine whether a change in process worked or not. For example, at Glen Cove Hospital the teams tested what they called Code Sepsis, a plan to get a clinical team with antibiotics and fluids to the bedside of a patient diagnosed with sepsis as quickly as possible. "We tried this and watched it for several days and got immediate feedback," says D'Angelo. "Some of the IV sizes weren't readily available and so we had the idea to make a 'go bag' with all of the IV fluid, tubing, catheters and blood tubes needed in the case of a Code Sepsis. We tested that and found that no one brought the bag! So we said, 'okay, it's the tech's job to get the 'go bag' and bring it to the patient's room.' We kept fine-tuning in that way."

"In any improvement project, success begets success," says Doerfler. "People start to see something that is achieving results. It is not just frustration. 'Why am I doing this? Oh, this is getting better.' Other people see something happening with success and somebody getting a pat on the back because they are doing a good job. They would like to join in and be part of the success. So you have reinforced that structural change."

In addition to the overall task force led by Doerfler, D'Angelo and Parmentier, there were also individual task forces established in each of the system's hospitals to focus on sepsis improvement. The initial task of defining sepsis, agreeing upon a treatment plan and measurement for that treatment had gone well. Now came the harder part—taking the essential template that had been developed and spreading it to every part of every hospital. Data revealed reality and the reality was that in too many instances Northwell teams were not doing what they thought they were doing. This was a job for Kathy Gallo and her simulation team at the Center for Learning and Innovation. Gallo had started out in health care as a nurse and she had worked for some years in an emergency department and seen firsthand how devastating sepsis could be. She also knew that conveying the new sepsis protocol to hundreds of doctors and a couple of thousand nurses throughout the system would require an organized educational initiative. She applied to the federal government for a Taming Sepsis Educational Program grant and received enough funding to set up a program to teach the new approach to nurses (and later doctors). The program included online learning as well as work within the Northwell simulation center where clinical teams were placed under increasingly stressful sessions where a mannequin simulated a variety of conditions that in some cases, though not all, suggested the possible presence of sepsis.

Sepsis Mortality Cut in Half

In the early years of the work, "we saw a narrowing of the variability and what looked like a change but it was the denominator effect," says Doerfler. "We are identifying more people so the number of people you are dividing the deaths over has grown, but the numbers of deaths aren't changing. It looks like you are getting better but you are not." But in 2012, things changed and the mortality rate began declining. By 2016 the results were definitive: *Mortality from sepsis within the system was more than cut in half from 31 percent in 2009 to 12 percent in 2016.* The improvement has been life-saving for thousands of people. The results were energizing to staff members, says Doerfler, who could see that "the fact that I did those things better is translating into really achieving why I am a healthcare professional either a doctor, a nurse, respiratory therapist, or anybody else. Those are really the key elements of the story as to this unfolding and its continuation into today. It really doesn't get any better than that."

The goal was to spread that practice throughout all Northwell hospitals so that in every emergency department on every shift doctors and nurses were following the Northwell ED Sepsis algorithm in a highly reliable, sustainable way. "The bundles that were published via the Surviving Sepsis Campaign addressed severe sepsis/shock not true early sepsis," says D'Angelo. "In these sepsis algorithms the goal was delivery of antibiotics and IV [fluids] within the first three hours after identification. What we did was set a very aggressive stretch goal to go along with our new ED algorithm that addressed the full spectrum (Sepsis, Severe Sepsis and Septic Shock). These stretch goals were to deliver antibiotics within 60 minutes and *initiate* the IV fluids within 30 minutes of time zero. The point was, although very aggressive and not evidence based, 'if we chase perfection we might catch excellence,' to quote Vince Lombardi. By setting the aggressive stretch goals, measuring them, and tracking progress toward hitting them, we began to see the numbers really move in the right direction."[6]

One of the unsettling aspects of health care in the modern world is the irrational way care is so often compensated. As we noted earlier, there is a shift underway from traditional fee-for-service payment to value-based payments; from paying for every little step along the way to paying for quality outcomes that benefit the patient. Doerfler notes that in the sepsis arena "if we are less than perfect, we get more revenue. If we are perfect, we get less revenue because people are less sick and we get paid on how sick they are. Even if they get sick because we did not provide good care, we get paid for it. But because they are less sick, we are also spending less. So we are saving society money. We are saving society lives and organ injury." One of the most important lessons involved the efficacy of the attitude and level of commitment at Northwell in the sepsis work. In a journal article, Doerfler et al. wrote that

> Our results suggest acknowledging sepsis as a time-dependent, high-consequence emergency warranting highly aggressive management is a clinical imperative. Our bundle accomplishes this, and importantly, several of our bundle elements are more aggressive than current recommendations. However, as evidenced by our strict compliance definition and observed mortality across both groups, we believe *this underlying attitude* to be as crucial a driver of survival benefit as any individual bundle component, and arguably the most important inference we draw from this investigation.

This underlying attitude was not measurable in the way you could calculate the time it took to get antibiotics into a patient, but its origin was clear. It came from Dowling when he initially saw sepsis results that were not good enough; from the Merinoff symposium; from the research both Kevin Tracey and Marty Doerfler had done earlier in their careers; and it came from the story of Rory Staunton.

"We are doing this. *I know it's wrong."*

From his "just shoot me" moment seven years ago, Doerfler and his colleagues have come a long way. In 2015 Northwell won the John M. Eisenberg Award for Patient Safety and Quality[7] given by the National Quality Forum and the Joint Commission. In a summary of the work for the *Joint Commission Journal on Quality and Patient Safety,* Doerfler and colleagues noted that sepsis mortality was reduced by 50 percent "by engaging leadership; fostering inter-professional collaboration, including with other leading health care organizations; and developing meaningful, real-time metrics for all levels of staff." In 2016, Doerfler was lauded as a "Sepsis Hero" by the Sepsis Alliance,[8] an organization founded by a dentist whose 23 year old daughter died of sepsis.

The work at Northwell has expanded beyond Emergency Departments and Critical Care units to include in-patient floors. Again, it is complicated and small changes can make a big difference. The fight against sepsis is humbling wherever the work takes place. And while it is tempting to feel a sense of accomplishment at progress to date, the Northwell teams never forget that anything less than constant vigilance is insufficient. They are surely humbled knowing that the words of Dr. Jeremy Boal, former chief medical officer at Northwell, remain true. Referring to Rory's case, Boal told *The New York Times*: "I think it could have happened almost anywhere. It absolutely could have happened here."[9]

For all the progress this remains a day-to-day, shift-to-shift challenge. Several times each year, the sepsis teams from all the Northwell hospitals gather to report on progress (or lack thereof in some places at some times) and to exchange ideas for improvement. These are energizing meetings for the most part where emergency room teams and inpatient teams report on some important advances. But then there is the other side of the coin—the humbling side. After all the progress it is sobering to be reminded that there are pockets within the system where breakdowns occur. Doerfler says that sometimes in these sessions "somebody stands up and says, 'in our place, we are doing *this*,' and jaws drop because the person will say, 'I know it's wrong.' They admit it's wrong and ask for help. We didn't do that before but we have become comfortable admitting that we don't know what we are doing. I am a doctor. We just do not do that." But the ability to do it is now embedded within the learning culture where people have "become self-aware and self-critical and then self-correcting."

Rory's Legacy

The Rory Staunton Foundation for Sepsis Prevention[10] aims "to ensure that no other child or young adult dies of sepsis resulting from the lack of a speedy diagnosis and immediate medical treatment." The Foundation mission is to reduce sepsis mortality by "raising public awareness of sepsis through education and awareness programs to promote faster diagnosis and effective treatment for children and young adults; Improving medical diagnosis of sepsis, particularly pediatric sepsis, through the implementation of rapid treatment protocols and improved communication between parents and medical staff in hospitals and medical clinics; and by supporting those affected by sepsis and providing a platform for their voices to be heard." [Doerfler serves on the foundation's three-member medical advisory board.]

In 2013, New York Governor Andrew Cuomo announced a set of regulations requiring all New York hospitals to adopt a set of best practices for identifying and treating sepsis. No other state had ever taken this step. There are no precise measurements for human suffering but, for a parent, the loss of a child brings on a level of grief that goes to a place that no human being should ever be. One theme among many of those parents is the desire to do something to keep the memory of the child alive and, in so doing, help other people. It is estimated that the new regulations, based largely on the type of best practices established at Northwell, have the potential to save anywhere from 5000 to 8000 lives per year.

Dr. D'Angelo remembers well when he heard about Rory's death in *The New York Times*. He read the article and emailed it to the entire sepsis team at Northwell seeking "to drive the point home that this is why we are working so hard on this issue. Soon, Michael Dowling connected with the family and we then started conducting meetings with the family—Marty, Darlene, myself and other colleagues. And based on those meetings we became involved as they advocated for state regulations to both aid in the fight to reduce death from sepsis and create safety checks, analogous to the stop signs on the sides of school buses, to mandate a pause in the Emergency Department management of children. This was to make sure all required due diligence in the work up was complete; all labs were back and parents were fully informed of what the diagnosis was, and, more importantly, what to watch for and what signs or new symptoms should be considered an urgent need to come back for re-evaluation. It was this second effort, for which we developed a process, that later became the foundation of the New York state Pediatric regulations and our sepsis effort and results are a key component of those regulations."

"Rory's Regulations," as promulgated by the state, require all hospitals in the state of New York "to adopt evidence-based protocols for the early diagnosis and treatment of sepsis;" protocols that essentially match what the Northwell teams have done. Cuomo also issued an additional set of regulations focused on ways "to improve quality and oversight of care provided to pediatric patients, including provisions to strengthen the ability of parents to play a meaningful and informed role in a child's healthcare decisions. Specifically, the regulations announced will newly require hospitals to implement procedures to ensure that parents and primary care providers receive key information about children's care, particularly by facilitating the communication of key tests and lab results."[11]

A Mother's Plea

Rory's mother, Orlaith Staunton, wrote an article,[12] which read, in part:

> Rory could have been saved, my son Rory could have been saved. I get a pain in my heart every time I think about that, which is all the time. Every day I remind myself that we are not waiting for a cure for sepsis the way we are waiting for a cure for cancer. Sepsis is preventable and treatable if found early and treated with broad spectrum antibiotics and IV fluids, that's all. At the time I didn't know to ask "could Rory have sepsis?" and none of the medical professionals I entrusted with his care thought about sepsis even though he had all the signs and they should have known.
>
> The signs of sepsis are broad, and often mimic flu like symptoms including fever, chills, pain, shortness of breath, mottled skin and dizziness. Parents, caregivers and educators have to learn to look for these signs and to think about sepsis so they can notice if "something is different" and ask about sepsis.
>
> After Rory's death I searched for information on what had killed my son and came up empty handed. The Centers for Disease Control (CDC) didn't list

sepsis on its website. I couldn't believe there was something out there that killed so many Americans; one person dies of sepsis every two minutes in the United States … it is also the biggest killer of children worldwide and it wasn't even mentioned on the CDC's website.

My husband Ciaran and I set up the Rory Staunton Foundation for Sepsis Prevention (www.rorystauntonfoundation.com). Our mission is to spare other families the pain and heartbreak that we have endured. In 2013, we succeeded in getting mandatory sepsis protocols adopted in New York State saving between 5,000 and 8,000 lives every year. We lobbied the CDC and in August, four years after Rory's death, they deemed sepsis a "medical emergency." We set up the National Family Council on Sepsis to act as a support and advocacy network for families of sepsis and we created a public education program about knowing the signs of sepsis. Our work is ongoing; this past weekend I heard from a mom who was on her way to pick up her seventeen year old daughter's autopsy report. The cause of death was sepsis. She asked me, "How come I didn't know the signs?"

Please take the time to talk about sepsis to others, I wish someone had talked about sepsis to me and I believe my son would be alive today if I had known the signs of sepsis.

Endnotes

1. "An Infection, Unnoticed, Turns Unstoppable," Jim Dwyer, *The New York Times*, July 11, 2012.
2. [*] German Sepsis Society; http://www.sepsis-gesellschaft.de/DSG/Englisch/Disease+pattern+of+Sepsis/Sepsis+History?sid=c7LtKgPZMy8MPKfuPqTGj0&iid=2.

3. "Sepsis is a life threatening condition that arises when the body's response to an infection injures its own tissues and organs. Sepsis leads to shock, multiple organ failure and death especially if not recognized early and treated promptly. Sepsis remains the primary cause of death from infection despite advances in modern medicine, including vaccines, antibiotics and acute care. Millions of people die of sepsis every year worldwide."

4. "Host-derived molecules and foreign products of infection converge on molecular mechanisms that cause unbalanced activation of innate immunity. Foreign and endogenous molecules interact with pathogen recognition receptors expressed on or in cells of the immune system. Activation of pathogen recognition receptors culminates in the release of immune mediators that produce the clinical signs and symptoms of sepsis."

5. Clinical Excellence Commission; http://www.cec.health. nsw.gov.au/quality-improvement/improvement-academy/ quality-improvement-tools/driver-diagrams.

6. (The average time to delivering antibiotics was in the range of 200-plus minutes in the early days of the task force. It improved to between 160–180 minutes after the rollout of the new Emergency Department sepsis algorithm and then improved to a system average of 80–90 minutes after setting aggressive stretch goals.)

7. Other winners included Mark Graber and the American College of Surgeons, as reported in the April issue of *Hospital Peer Review*.

8. care.http://www.sepsisalliance.org/sepsis_heroes/ martin_doerfler/.

9. "Death of a Boy Prompts New Medical Efforts Nationwide;" About New York By Jim Dwyer, Oct. 25, 2012; http://www. nytimes.com/2012/10/26/nyregion/tale-of-rory-stauntons-death-prompts-new-medical-efforts-nationwide.html.

10. https://rorystauntonfoundationforsepsis.org/ about-our-foundation-2/.

11. The regulations proposed by the state "require hospitals to develop and implement policies and procedures to:
    – Ensure that all test results are reviewed upon completion by a physician, physician assistant or nurse practitioner;

- Ask the identity of a patient's primary care provider, if any, on admission, and forward all test results to that primary care provider;
- Prohibit the discharge of a patient until test results that may reasonably be expected to yield "critical values" indicating a life-threatening or other condition requiring immediate medical attention are completed and communicated; and
- Communicate prior to discharge all categories of tests ordered, all critical value test results, and what, if any, (non-critical) tests are still pending; and
- Carry out such communication in plain, understandable terms to the patient or the patient's parent or medical decision-maker, as appropriate. The pediatric regulations also will make other key reforms to the delivery of pediatric care, such as requiring hospitals to:
- Enable parents or guardians to stay with pediatric patients while they are receiving care, including to permit at least one parent or guardian to remain with the pediatric patient at all times;
- Ensure that hospitals admitting children have appropriate staff, resources and age-appropriate equipment and establish policies and procedures for transferring children when needed and appropriate."

12. "I am a mother who lost a child who could have been saved …;" *Huffington Post*, November 23, 2016.

Chapter 8

Care Value

"We have to be focused on keeping people well rather than just treating them when they are sick."

Michael Dowling

"Quality had nothing to do with it."

In most areas of commerce, products and services are paid for based on volume, with a generally fixed price for each quart of milk, each book, each home appliance purchased. Transactions in the service industry are similar: You pay a certain amount every time the lawn care service comes by to mow the grass or each time you get a haircut. This fee-for-service approach has long been the main method of payment within health care. For doctors, this always meant that the greater the volume of their work the more they were paid. But that is changing and the scale and complexity of that change presents the health care industry with an uncomfortable and often awkward challenge. "We are moving from a world where you get paid to just do more stuff to getting paid because what you did produced a quality outcome," says Dr. Lawrence Smith, Northwell Physician-in-Chief and Dean of the Hofstra Northwell School of Medicine. "That is radically different. During my years practicing medicine I got paid the exact same amount if I

171

made a mistake and harmed a patient as if I saved somebody's life. It made no difference. Quality had nothing to do with it." Amazing! Amazing to consider that the quality of care delivered by a doctor through the years had little or no bearing on compensation. Only volume mattered. A hernia operation that results in a hospital acquired infection? Hospital and surgeon receive full payment for the operation and the hospital would often get paid more due to the higher complexity of care needed to treat the infection. In the new world, instead of being paid on the basis of examinations performed and procedures completed, doctors will be paid for keeping patients chronic conditions under control; for making sure patients use the Emergency Department as *infrequently* as possible; for keeping their patients *out* of the hospital. This shift can be described as essentially a change from paying exclusively for sick care services to paying for *health and patient-important outcomes*—promoting activities that further well-being in care settings comfortable for patients and families. It is a world turned upside down—from a time not so long ago when a way to make money for a provider was to admit as many patients to the hospital as possible to a time now when the opposite is often true. "We have to be focused on keeping people well," says Michael Dowling, "rather than just treating them when they are sick."

"As long as I keep you healthy and you are satisfied, we are having a good relationship."

Has there ever been a more turbulent time in the world of health care? A time when some of the most foundational elements of the business—how care is delivered and paid for—were undergoing such fundamental change? Hospitals and physician groups are dealing with a radically altered landscape at the same time that both government and private insurers are squeezing payments at every level. The tug-of-war over every dollar in health care has never been fiercer. Insurance companies jealously guard the dollars they collect and work to drive down the prices they pay to doctors and hospitals for medical services. On the other side of the ledger, hospitals and physician groups struggle to adapt to decreasing payments even as pressure mounts to produce measurably improved outcomes for patients.

This era of downward revenue pressures increases the already contentious relationships between provider organizations and insurance companies. Howard Gold, Northwell Executive Vice President, has been the point man on negotiations with insurance companies on behalf of Northwell hospitals and doctors since 1995. In these negotiations, says Gold, "there is always tension and there is always acrimony and there is always suspicion." The challenge is that often the negotiations are a zero-sum game for providers and surely that is often true in fee-for-service contracts.

The new payment method presents a culture shock for many physicians. "I grew up in the world of billable events," says Dr. Smith. "If you did not create a billable event, you were giving away your expertise for nothing. Why should I ever treat you over the phone? I spent 15 years of my life becoming an expert physician. Why should I give away my knowledge over the phone for free when I cannot bill you for that? Now, we are going to go into a world where all of that is irrelevant. Somebody is going to pay me a number of dollars per month to be your doctor whether I see you every day or once a year. As long as I keep you healthy and you are satisfied, we are having a good relationship. I do not need to create an event I can bill you for every time you have a problem because I do not bill you anymore. I am getting paid to take care of you. We have got to find a way to legitimately reward people when their model of care has a whole bunch of things that you traditionally cannot bill for." As a primary care physician for many years, Smith estimates that he could have treated about one out of every five acute problems over the phone but if he had done so he would not have been paid. There was no compensation from insurance companies for a phone call. Never mind that he might have solved the patient's problem quickly and skillfully. Never mind that the patient would be happy and healthier. Payment was for activities such as an office visit, physical exam, or surgical procedure regardless of whether these steps had any impact on the patient's health or well-being. You were paid for doing things. If Dr. Smith had been paid a lump sum to take care of a defined patient population, however, he could treat maybe as many as 20 percent of the time without a face-to-face encounter—greater convenience for the patient and in all like-lihood, better outcomes.

As health care moves through the current transition period, doctors have one foot on the dock and one in the boat. As a physician, should you follow insurance company procedures to the letter in order to get paid, or, for example, do you provide great care over the phone while the patient is safely home—doing clearly what is best for the patient—yet not creating a billable event for insurance? This dilemma fuels the uncertainty among physicians. Will they be paid on a piece-work basis or will reimbursement models change so they are paid in advance on a fixed monthly fee per patient? There are pros and cons to each methodology. And, to add to the complexity, for the foreseeable future it seems likely that pay-ment will involve some combination of both approaches. The advocates for fixed payment approach argue that when paid in advance the doctor can focus on a patient's health with-out worrying about the complexities of insurance company rules and policies. Dowling acknowledges the complexity but believes moving toward population health management will produce better results for patients, payers and providers. "We want to move to a system whereby you're responsible for the holistic management of a person's health and get paid and have the ability to do prevention, wellness promotion, have people taken care of in the appropriate location and not nec-essarily have everybody going to a hospital."

While Gold, who negotiates the Northwell contracts with insurers, agrees in principle with Dowling and Smith, to take the "piecework" model and turn it into an overall healthcare payment, flashes yellow caution lights. Are we ready? Can providers manage a whole person? Can providers and payers enter into partnerships and share data about large populations? Virtually every contract Northwell lift with payers includes some portion of the payment that is value-based, though in most of those contracts that portion is a small percent. Gold emphasizes that he is moving "deliberately, gradually, cautiously" toward these risk-based contracts "until we are better capable of sharing risk and being paid on outcomes and quality metrics." And a necessary condition of such a shift, he says, "is shared data and an agreement among all providers to use evidence-based medicine." If a contract pays Northwell $500 per month per person to take care of a large population of patients (the employees of a particular company, for example), Gold sees a progressive scenario. At the start, if Northwell is able to take care of that patient for $450 per month, Gold sees splitting that saved $50 between Northwell and the insurance company, splitting losses in a similar fashion. In three years or so, says Gold, he may feel Northwell's risk management capability is such that Northwell might assume risk for the "whole population—100,000 lives times $500 per person per month and we will take risk on everything. We wouldn't want to move fully to risk before we had an effective ambulatory care continuum and a very effective management service organization and a group of primary care doctors who are absolutely committed to managing the population." In reality, those elements are developing quickly throughout Northwell. There is a robust ambulatory care network, a growing care management capability, and increasing numbers of primary care physicians willing to make the leap. While many doctors are uncomfortable with the change, Smith says the shift from fee-for-service to value based payment could have a positive effect on the way they practice. "The one wonderful thing we know is really good doctors delivering really good care are almost universally low cost," says Smith. "Really smart

doctors delivering really good care to patients is almost always
a conservative model of spending. They have judgment. They
trust their judgment. They are smart. They do not endlessly do
tests just to reassure themselves when they know the tests are
irrelevant. They are busy. They do not do unnecessary stuff
because they do not need to make business for themselves
because the really good doctors are all busy. The trick is to
reward the people who are doing it right and nudge the other
people along. You cannot mandate it."

On its face, the notion of changing the way health care is
paid for, is a watching paint dry exercise. In fact, it allows for
the reinvention of the industry and presents an historic opportunity to push toward the real mission. "I want to be in the
health business, the health promotion business, the wellness
business, as well as the illness care business," says Dowling. "I
want to be able to do all those things well. To do that, we have
to have the right structures, the right delivery components, the
right alignment of incentives and the right partnerships. For
those who are willing to be creative, for those who are looking
to innovate, it is a great time to be in health care." As powerful
as the trend away from fee-for-service and toward value based
payments is at the moment, Mark Solazzo offers a cautionary
note. "We don't know exactly where health care reimbursement
is going," he says. "We would like it to continue to go in this
direction but we do not know for sure. Things can change and
we have to have the ability to prosper in any payment system."

"That reduction in suffering also happens to yield better financial performance within this new construct."

All major provider organizations are moving toward value-
based contracts, albeit at varying rates of speed. The more
daring move—and certainly the riskier move—is to start a
new insurance company, which is precisely what Dowling
did. He watched for years as insurance companies took in
hundreds of millions of dollars. With the amount of money

government and employers are willing to pay for health care declining, would it be possible for Northwell to claim some of the money going to insurance companies? To do so, the organization would have to provide strong management for the health of populations of patients. "The question," says Dowling, "was how do we get a piece of the premium so that we are managing not the episode of care with someone coming in for a particular service, but rather taking responsibility for the care of an entire population of people over a period of years? And one of the ways to do that is organize ourselves and our financing vehicle and our provider vehicle to take risk; to go to the insurance companies and say, 'we will take care of everybody who signs up with one of our doctors or in our geography and we will provide all the services they need—hospitalization, hospice care, birth care, you name it we will do it all at a percentage of the premium'." As he noted in a piece on the Health Affairs Blog: "The answer goes back to being in the 'health' business. We want to have as much control as possible over the premium dollar so that we can manage people's health and not just manage people's illnesses. That way, when we reduce the utilization in a hospital, we get to keep some of the savings. The old model was a terrible misalignment of incentives. We could do wonderful things to reduce hospital utilization, but if the insurance companies got the savings and left hospitals with the cost, where did that leave providers or their patients? By effectively being in the 'insurance business' and partnering in an insurance company, we can more appropriately align the incentives."

A New Company

Alan Murray, CEO of CareConnect, the Northwell insurance company, joined the organization in 2012, having had 10 years of experience in the insurance business in New York. Murray had seen the evolving health care world from his insurance company perch and he understood the intricacies of the shift from the fee-for-service payment environment to value-based payment. Soon after he arrived at Northwell, it became clear to Murray that the organization was well-positioned to take on the role of an insurer. "We had the reputation and scale to begin to think very differently than just the typical provider–payer relationship and so we started having conversations about going into the risk world," says Murray. This was tricky territory. Northwell, after all, was in the business of taking care of patients whether in the hospital, in an ambulance, or in an out-patient setting. If Northwell was to get into the insurance business it would have to do things that, as a provider group, it had never focused on before: Manage risk and underwrite and pay claims. This can be treacherous financial terrain. On the other side of the ledger Northwell did have experience with some insurance-related functions including customer service and medical management. The challenge was to align the two—get the care delivery and insurance functions to pull together in pursuit of a single, overriding goal. Others had done it, of course, perhaps most notably Kaiser Permanente based in California, whose pre-paid model had become a recognized standard of excellence. For Northwell to pull off starting and growing a new insurance company it also required the rather awkward dance involved in contracting with competitor hospitals and doctors to care for patients under the Northwell insurance plan. Even more uncomfortable, there was no template; no standard set of plans for a provider organization to build a new insurance company. This meant learning from what others had done—taking bits and pieces from here and there, but, ultimately, Dowling and team would have to build this new entity on their own using their knowledge of the local and regional health care scene. This would require specialized skills and, perhaps most unnerving, create significant financial risk for the organization. The timing was propitious, however. Provisions within the Affordable Care Act created an opportunity for the new insurance company to get off the ground quickly. The law essentially standardized benefit designs while adding millions of new people to the insurance marketplace. After Dowling gave Gold and Murray the green light to creating the insurance company, the new entity had a license by August 2013, and was accepting members at the start of 2014.

"The health outcomes achieved that matter to patients relative to the cost of achieving those outcomes."

Along with the creation of CareConnect came the birth of Health Solutions, a care management organization responsible for the implementation and performance of Northwell's value-based programs. Partnering with CareConnect, Health Solutions provides disease management for all CareConnect members including the task of managing the care of mostly older people with multiple, complex chronic conditions and doing so on a fixed payment typically from Medicare or Medicaid or both. The job of making this work fell to the team of Kris Smith, MD, senior vice president for population health and Medical Director for Northwell Health Solutions, and Joseph Schulman, Executive Director for Northwell Health Solutions. The two work in close partnership to manage the care—and the cost of care—for patients enrolled in CareConnect. The broader mission of Health Solutions is to take responsibility for Northwell's performance in value based payment arrangements. This is among the most urgent challenges in U.S. health care today and it requires managing high-risk patients to improve their health and control costs. Of all the work taking place at Northwell this is among the most humbling and perhaps the most promising. Over the long term, building programs that take good care of high risk, high cost patients is a necessity. Schulman brings a background in finance to the task and has focused a good deal of time on building an analytic capability within Health Solutions. Good data, carefully analyzed, says Schulman, provides important insights into risk stratification and predictive modeling that can make or break a population health initiative. Smith and

Schulman are drawn to the thinking of Harvard Professor Michael Porter, who defines value as "the health outcomes achieved that matter to patients relative to the cost of achieving those outcomes."[1] Schulman notes that he and Smith like Porter's definition for it goes to the heart of "what matters to patients, beneficiaries, providers, and what matters to families." Porter has collaborated on some of his writing with Thomas Lee, MD, Medical Director at Press Ganey, and an article that Lee authored in the *New England Journal of Medicine* contends that the language of health care—an "adverse event," for example—masks the harsh reality of human suffering. "We protect ourselves by these abstract words and these numbers and statistics but at its core these numbers tell a tale of unnecessary suffering," says Smith. Consider the case of a patient who has a knee surgically replaced, he says. Under a value-based contract, the goal is to get the patient home as quickly as possible—to avoid having to place the patient into a rehab facility after surgery which drives up the overall cost of care considerably. Smith argues that focus on the concept of patient suffering results in high quality, low cost care. "Think of how much less someone suffers being at home than they do in an unknown rehab facility," says Smith. "That reduction in suffering also yields better financial performance within this new construct." Smith argues that under new payment models there is alignment that less suffering for patients means better financial performance for the organization.

"I think we get too distanced from what's actually happening to the patient when a hospital has a bad readmission rate, for example," he says. "What a high readmission rate really represents is an enormous amount of unnecessary suffering on behalf of patients and families and if we can solve for that—if we can reduce that suffering and in this new world figure out a way to reap the financial rewards of that reduction or alleviation of suffering—then we have a great story to tell."

Smith trained in internal medicine with a particular focus on hospice and palliative care and when he thinks about reducing suffering among patients his thoughts naturally turn to older patients who tend to be frail and susceptible to unwanted and unpleasant outcomes. If you want to reduce suffering among those patients, says Smith, you have to *visit them at home* to see how they are doing and to take the steps needed to avert suffering before it sets in. Thus, the creation at Northwell of the House Calls program, an initiative to go back to the future of health care—house calls aligned with the latest payment methods. This goes to one of the fundamental issues in health care in the twenty-first century: *What works? What approaches deliver quality care at an affordable price?* Provider organizations are trying a variety of approaches. Most initiatives target "frequent fliers"—the estimated five percent of patients who account for about half of all health care spending. The House Calls program works in this space. Smith and his colleagues are focused intensively on about 1200 mostly elderly patients (average age mid-80s) who are afflicted with multiple chronic conditions and who also have difficulty leaving their homes to get to regular medical appointments which would help stabilize their conditions. "The functional impairment and medical complexity means these patients wind up in emergency rooms at high rates," says Smith. "Since they cannot get to traditional outpatient care, we bring the care to them." Each patient is cared for by a team that includes a physician working with nurses, nurse practitioners, a social worker, and support staff. Each team cares for about 150 patients at a time (versus 2000 or more patients that many primary care physicians have in their panels). "The program is all about high quality, highly reliable, time responsive care to a group of patients who are very frail and challenged to access medical care," says Smith. Some funding to support the initiative has come from a federal demonstration program (called "Independent at Home") which aims to determine whether home visits to elderly patients actually improve quality of care while reducing costs. Results from the first two years of the program show that it provides a high level of care to patients, and that this quality results in a decline in the total cost of care by as much as 25 percent in the highest performing practices.

The real challenge for Smith and Schulman is scaling this approach to larger populations of patients who are not as old and frail but who nonetheless suffer from multiple chronic conditions, have difficulty getting out to medical appointments, and rely too often on the high cost services of an emergency department. The scalability stumbles fairly quickly on the reality that there are only so many primary care physicians available to do this work. The trend within medical schools (including Hofstra Northwell) is for the overwhelming majority of students to select specialties other than primary care even as the baby boom generation of primary care doctors is quickly retiring. For the sake of efficiency and quality care, Smith is working to spare doctors from treating conditions that can be handled by others, reserving the most challenging cases—the ones where physician training is essential—for doctors. "When a patient who has multiple chronic illnesses is getting worse and may have pneumonia or heart failure, we want to make sure our physicians are free to respond to those cases, the ones that require the highest level of clinical reasoning," he says.

The primary care team plays the central role in caring for these patients, but the team members are not able to respond to all of the patients' needs all of the time. This is where a critical piece of the care management puzzle comes into play—a 24-hour clinical call center staffed by nurses. Most calls are resolved by nurses on duty, but there are still thousands of situations each year where the case cannot be handled by a nurse; where the facts of the case are too confusing to be handled on the phone. In these cases Northwell sends an ambulance to the home, but this is a different mindset than the standard ambulance experience where the paramedics arrive, stabilize the patient and then transport to the Emergency Room. This Community Paramedic Program (also known as Mobile Integrated Health) is specifically designed to deliver care in the home and to the greatest extent possible keep patients out of the ER. It is one of those rare cases in the U.S. where ambulance teams arrive at a home with the expressed goal of *not* taking the patient to the hospital. Paramedics are sent "out to the homes of these patients to do an evaluation," says Smith, and the paramedics understand that the goal of the primary care team is to keep the patients healthy and in their homes whenever possible. The paramedics have significant capabilities from their own training and experience, but they are also able to connect with a physician on voice or video conference. On video conferencing, the doctor can see the patient and make a treatment decision. *Emergency room or not? Okay, it's not the emergency room, we want to give them some oxygen, give them something for their heart failure.* As of spring 2016, the team had fielded 1200 calls with an average response time of 23 minutes. It is important to consider this in context. This is not getting an emergency crew to transport a patient in 23 minutes. Rather, *this is getting aligned members of a primary care team to the home and treating the patient in 23 minutes!* This is an example of finding excess capacity within a health care system that appears so often at the breaking point. Northwell paramedics are very busy, but not *always* busy and the down times are the opportunity to use the ambulance personnel as extenders for the primary care team integrated within the House Calls program.

Smith, Schulman, and their colleagues have invested significant time training staff to communicate effectively with patients—to speak with them in ways they understand so that staff can get patients, as Smith puts it, "to say yes;" yes to smoking cessation, weight loss, a wide variety of habits that are essential to improving health. "So everybody, whether you're a nurse, a social worker, a non-licensed professional, a physician you've got to figure out how to get patients to say yes," he says. "We can build exquisite programs but if nobody says yes, it doesn't matter how good the program is. Then once they say yes, how is it that you engage them, activate them, partner with them? How do you train patients to call our programs instead of 911 in a time of need? If we can build trust in the responsiveness of our clinical programs, patients won't feel the need to turn to the emergency room, resulting in better care at a lower total cost."

"It's ten years of hell to get this right."

As expected, the insurance company lost money during its first several years of operation. "The debate now is how much more capital do we need?" says Howard Gold. "How much more resources? How long will the losses be? Can we really sell? Because everybody else has a broad network and we have a narrow network. We priced ourselves lower than everybody else and that is why people are buying. That is a good thing, but you have to ask, is it priced too low? And it is not our core competence but the main thing to us is does it drive business, revenue and margin to us that we wouldn't get on our own and does it hurt our relationships with other payers."

In 2017, three years after its founding, the insurance entity had about 120,000 members, about $650 million in revenue, and about 300 employees. Decent, but dwarfed by major commercial insurers in the marketplace. While CareConnect is growing, it has encountered some heavy weather in the form of a $140 million hit to the bottom line based on an ill-conceived federal mandate. Here is how the unfortunate situation was conveyed by the insurance company to customers for 2017 concerning a rate increase:

> A number of factors have led CareConnect to seek a rate increase for group plans. Like other insurance companies, we have experienced an increase in the cost of providing health care services, due to factors like advances in technology and higher pharmacy costs, particularly for specialty drugs. *However, it is the unintended impact of the federal "Risk Adjuster" program that is driving the largest component of our increase. This program was designed to protect*

insurance companies that happen to enroll a higher-risk population; however, in practice, it penalizes small, start-up companies that lack historical data for their members.

CareConnect's 2015 liability under this program amounts to nearly one-third of the entire premium revenue we collected that year.

There is a lot of *what if* to CareConnect. What if losses continue? Could red ink threaten Northwell's core financial stability? On the brighter side, what if it continues to grow and achieves a scale that gets it to covering, say, a half million lives? At that point, it would be a serious player in the marketplace. Dowling is never opposed to hedging his bets and he was doing that at the very end of 2016 by discussing the possibility of a merger of CareConnect with larger insurance companies. "It is important to remember that if you look around the country at the health systems that do some of the best work and are the most successful they all have insurance companies, but they have been at it 30 years," he says. "You analyze any of them—Intermountain, Geisinger, others—they would tell you it's ten years of hell to get this right. We have to be very careful it doesn't cause a disruption that we can't handle. We've got to watch that very carefully. You have got to be able to ride it for a long period of time. What I would like to get to in five or six years is 500,000 or 600,000 members. Now you are relevant. Now you get attention."

While CareConnect is still modest in size, Dowling says it has nonetheless already "changed the culture of the organization in a big way by making us understand more than anything else that we have an accountability to only do those things that are right and not focus as much as we have traditionally done on the hospital side of the business but more on the ambulatory. It forces us to think more on how to go upstream and prevent problems before they start. And I think having that internal to the organization is very, very important in the long run." This goes to the Northwell core strategy around ambulatory care. A decade or so ago, about 90 percent of Northwell's revenue came from in-patient hospital stays. Since then, the evolution away from in-patient care to providing care in ambulatory settings has accelerated to the point where, within a year or two, half of all Northwell's revenue will come from ambulatory services.

The insurance company has been an important learning experience for the Northwell leadership team, says Solazzo. "The insurance company has made us think differently," he says. "It has taught us more about how to do care management in an ambulatory environment, how to do pilots toward better care, how to keep people out of the ED." The potential impact of the insurance company on the financial health of Northwell is hard to overstate. "You get the full premium now," says Dowling. "If you manage it right you get to keep the money. Today, in the absence of that, when I do things to manage care well I don't get any of the benefit. I lose money. You have an inherent conflict in the organization. In the current fee-for-service construct, for us to be successful we have to have our hospitals full, yet new payment models are encouraging us to take people out of the hospital and serve them in an expanded and more technically proficient ambulatory care setting. So you are dealing with a great paradox. I can keep people out of the hospital today more than I am, but the only people I make richer are Empire Blue Cross, Aetna, United and all the other insurers—who do not have the responsibility of actually treating people."

Among the more surprising effects of the insurance company's growth within the organization is that, increasingly, people within Northwell—doctors, nurses, administrators—feel an ever greater sense of responsibility for the overall well-being of patients. "We have 100,000 people who have put their trust in Northwell, not on an episodic basis or on a one time basis," says Murray, but rather in a broader context where Northwell is taking responsibility for the health of these individuals and families. "Because we have responsibility for this population, which is obviously growing, the whole system now feels the responsibility of this family we've created. This has had a very positive impact in the way the leadership looks at that population. The way that we can now begin to apply those lessons to other businesses outside of just the insurance functions, so for example, if the health system has some sort of risk arrangement with another payer, the infrastructure that has been created by CareConnect to manage that population and all of the other stuff around it can now begin to be applied to managing the population over here."

"Right now providers are very good at managing a patient but managing a population" is a different matter entirely, says Murray. "Number one you've got to have a strategy but then you have to have the know-how to actually impact that population to change behavior, focusing on managing the five percent. The five percent need care and you're going to have an individual program for each one of them which is essentially saving money."

Says Howard Gold: "Our goal is to inspire confidence in the health system that it really can transform itself from a piecework, fee-for-service mentality to a population-based framework that pays us for producing better outcomes for individual patients."

Endnote

1. The Strategy That Will Fix Health Care by Michael E. Porter and Thomas H. Lee, MD; October 2013 HBR; Thomas H. Lee, MD, is the chief medical officer at Press Ganey Associates. He is the co-author of the HBR article Engaging Doctors in the Health Care Revolution and An Epidemic of Empathy in Health Care (McGraw-Hill 2015).

Chapter 9

Beyond the Horizon

"I don't think anyone knows yet how far this can go."

Dr. Lawrence Smith

The Road Ahead

Michael Dowling strains to peer over the horizon, to try and fathom where the business of health care is headed. He needs to understand what the future pathway looks like if he is to deliver on the real mission, but it is not easy to see through the fog that enshrouds so much of this vast industry with its opaque images and blind spots. Dowling makes no pretension that he sees everything, but he does see enough to know that the path forward is uncertain, like one of those crazy video games where the landscape suddenly shifts and peril is everywhere.

Up ahead, Dowling sees the good, the bad, and the ugly. He sees as many questions as answers, but he also sees some amazing opportunities. The bad/ugly side of the ledger presents itself clearly. Here Dowling sees complacency and self-satisfaction in some corners of the business and he worries about it infecting his own organization. When things go well, as they have at Northwell, human nature can nudge people into self-satisfaction. He worries that the ideas which seemed so fresh yesterday might go stale tomorrow. "Complacency is a trap and you need to innovate and change to fight it," he says. "If you aren't constantly encouraging innovation efforts, you risk falling into the complacency trap and once you've fallen in it's quite difficult to get out."

He worries that sometimes there is too much focus on delivering medical services and not on *health* per se. This is the hardest nut of all to crack and Dowling knows it. He sees the Sisyphean task of caring for Vincent and all the Vincents of the world; these patients with multiple, complex chronic conditions often including behavioral health issues comprise about 10 percent of the population yet account for nearly two-thirds of all health care spending.[1] He wants his teams to act more aggressively on the determinants of health that happen outside the clinic. To accelerate Northwell's work in this area Dowling hired Dr. Ram Raju, former head of the nation's largest public health system, New York Health + Hospitals. At Northwell, Dr. Raju is exploring ways to deliver care to improve population health overall and target the social determinants of health for all patients including those in the New York area's most-vulnerable communities. Dowling knows this is *the* challenge in health care in the country today yet he cannot help but be impatient. At a meeting with his senior team recently he was blunt: "We have to raise the bar," he told them. "We still have too much variation on clinical stuff. We have integrated well and set common metrics, but we haven't dealt with the variations that exist. We don't do the service piece as well as we should. We have to see ourselves as a health organization other than being the medical organization. We are too confined by medicine. Sometimes I think doctors know the science of medicine but not an awful lot about health."

On the negative side of the ledger, he sees disruption and confusion that will continue as defining characteristics of American health care. Of this he is sure and the current turbulence requires an ability to operate calmly amid the turbulence. The truth is that Dowling is not uncomfortable in this swirl of chaos and he is convinced that people in health care who demand clarity will not fare well. Although his roots are in government where he oversaw many different regulations, Dowling simmers with frustration as he looks ahead and sees little hope that the burden of regulation will ease. "I am by no means anti-regulation, but we are inundated with micro-regulations that make the business much more complicated than it needs to be, consume money and time, and only marginally improve outcomes for patients." He sees a period ahead where regulation will continue to impede innovation and progress.

Clearly visible to Dowling and everyone else in health care is increasing consolidation, with provider groups growing ever larger with more doctors, more hospitals joining forces to the point where, at a time in the not too distant future, "there won't be any small entities left." While it is easy to see the continuing trend, it is more challenging to parse out exactly what the result will be. Will consolidation produce enormous provider entities that dominate to such an extent that they consume even more resources, fattening their bottom lines by demanding ever higher payments from insurance companies, employers and individuals? Or will these larger groups have the aligned resources necessary to improve the health and well-being of entire communities while controlling costs? In other words, to deliver on the promise of the real mission? In certain markets, dominant players will consolidate to leapfrog so far ahead that they control market prices with the monopolistic result that quality will decline while costs rise. The theoretical promise of consolidation is the ability of large players to coordinate care, deliver it in the right location, and address determinants of health—all toward improving overall health while controlling costs. The truth is no one yet knows which organizations in which marketplaces will follow the former path and which will follow the later.

For all of these obstacles ahead there is a positive side to the ledger that energizes Dowling. For example, he sees the accelerating evolution of the way health care is paid for, from fee-for-service and toward a value based approach where doctors and hospitals are given a fixed amount of money to take care of patients. This is a most welcome vision for Dowling for he believes that Northwell is building a foundation upon which to thrive under such an approach; an integrated continuum of care covering all patient needs. "We want to move to a system whereby you are responsible for the holistic management of a person's health and that is what you are paid for so you have the ability to do prevention, wellness promotion, have people taken care of in the appropriate location and not necessarily have everybody going to a hospital." Dowling sees the move from hospitals to ambulatory settings and this is the direction in which the Northwell ship is headed as rapidly as the engine room pistons can churn. And he sees the need—the compulsion really—to stretch and reach for great breakthroughs, for the medical miracles that change the nature of health in society.

You are part of the problem. Are you part of the solution?

Before making his way over that horizon, Dowling must deal with the reality of the present. While the future is more difficult to discern than Dowling would like, he has no trouble seeing what is real today. He is well aware that the finest medical care ever devised by humans today enables tens of millions of people to live longer, healthier lives. This scientific magic, however, happens within a massive, unwieldy monster of a system. But it is, as Dowling notes, "a crisis not of failure but of success. People are living 35 years longer today than people born in 1900. The problem is we're having trouble affording it."

It is this reality that is perhaps best described by one of the most commonly used words in the modern health care lexicon: *Unsustainable*. Spend time in health care today and you will hear the word "unsustainable" used again and again. What does this mean, exactly? For one thing it means that health care is seizing an ever growing share of the Gross Domestic Product thus reducing funds available for everything else—infrastructure improvement, education, environmental protection, national defense, etc. While the economy was limping along at an anemic rate of under 2 percent in 2015, spending on health care in the United States grew 5.8 percent to more than $3 trillion. This works out to an average cost of a few dollars shy of $10,000 *per person* in the U.S.

Perhaps the most painful definition of *unsustainable* comes when we move from the macro world into the micro world Dowling knows well; from the national numbers to the kitchen table where families try and make ends meet. A RAND Corporation analysis[2] found that spending on health care "nearly doubled between 1999 and 2009. This increase has substantially eroded what an average family has left to spend on everything else, leaving them with only $95 more per month than in 1999. Had health care costs tracked the rise in the Consumer Price Index, rather than outpacing it, an average American family would have had an additional $450 per month—*more than $5,000 per year*—to spend on other priorities." The RAND analysis "demonstrates that over the past decade, health care cost growth has consumed a large share of the disposable income of the average American family [while also] … adding to the federal budget deficit." Dowling wonders when the backlash will come? When will teachers, construction workers, environmentalists, and others recognize that the voracious appetite of the health care industry for money is hurting them? Less than a dozen years ago, health care was a $2 trillion industry and it wanted more and now it is a $3 trillion industry and it wants still more.

What does this have to do with Michael Dowling and his colleagues? Everything. For the present, reality arrives at the front
door of Northwell Health every morning and from Dowling's
perspective if you are in the health care business you are part
of the problem. That holds true whether you are a hospital or
physician group, device manufacturer, insurance or pharmaceutical company. That you are part of the problem is undeniable.
The question going forward is: *Are you part of the solution?*

You can only be part of the solution if you have a strategy that gets you toward the equity-quality-affordability
equation. In some measure, that means delivering as much
care as possible outside major academic medical centers in
the ambulatory world as near to the patient as possible. A
hospital is an ideal place for someone very sick in need of
intensive, highly professionalized care. Increasingly, however,
procedures and treatments formerly exclusive to hospitals
are delivered in ambulatory settings. At Northwell, in-patient
care accounted for nearly 70 percent of revenue (30 percent
from outpatient) as recently as 2005, but by 2017 in-patient
was down to 56 percent of budgeted revenues (with outpatient at 44 percent). Hospitals are critically important to the
Northwell strategy going forward but they are not the core of
that strategy. Actually, the core of the strategy is delivering as
much care as possible outside of hospitals; partnering with
community physicians and developing an ambulatory infrastructure which includes facilities scattered throughout the
communities for urgent care, ambulatory-surgery and dialysis, and freestanding emergency departments. This vision of
a large, community-based ambulatory-focused health system
goes back to the 1990s when Dowling, Mark Solazzo, Howard
Gold and others were working for the state government.
"We believed in setting up provider networks with primary
care doctors as a central piece and hospitals were really big
and very often we were considered anti-hospital because we
wanted money from the hospitals to build ambulatory care to

build primary care," says Gold. "We thought patients could be taken care of by primary care physicians and they would coordinate the care. And if it was going to the appropriate place then money could be used more effectively and efficiently and then you could cover more people."

Ambulatory care includes the kind of outreach prevention and wellness that advances the health agenda. In this context Dowling has written that "a simple but important question faces all providers. Do we understand the difference between medical delivery and health? Those who do—and see themselves in the 'health business'—will succeed as the industry transforms. Those who do not—and remain only in the 'hospital business'—will ... struggle to survive."[3]

> The reason for this is that the health business is not just about the hospital business anymore. That reality has been difficult for some providers to grasp. Do we need hospitals? Yes. When you get really sick or experience a serious injury, you need hospitals. When you have a chronic condition, you may need hospitals—although we are getting better at successfully managing the care of chronically ill patients in their homes or community-based settings. Hospitals do great things. They provide phenomenal service. But they are not, nor were they ever intended to be, wholly synonymous with health care.
>
> With advances in science and technology, most surgery can be performed less expensively and just as safely outside of a hospital. The expansion of ambulatory services, urgent care centers, and free-standing emergency rooms has dramatically reduced the utilization of hospitals. Compared to a decade ago, between 30 and 40 percent of the procedures traditionally performed in medical centers can now be done in ambulatory settings.

"Telehealth for any patient anywhere for any need."

Thomas Thornton, senior vice president of Northwell Ventures, spends a lot of time studying advances in technology and practice which advance ambulatory care and Thornton finds that throughout the health care universe there is a constant buzz about ambulatory strategies. Buzz notwithstanding, however, as Thornton works his way around the country he sees few well-evolved ambulatory strategies. "Most entities revolve around the mother ship," he says, "and the attitude in these places is, 'we're the campus. We want everyone to come to the campus. If you live five miles away, you come here. If you live fifty miles away, you come here'."

An ambulatory strategy takes essentially the opposite approach so that in every case possible care is delivered as close to the patient as possible. Delivering care in a patient's home is the ideal in many cases and this aspiration will be a reality in the next couple of years with the growing sophistication of telemedicine. In its current form, telemedicine already connects patients in various locations with specialists. For example, emergency department physicians regularly encounter patients with behavioral issues who would benefit from psychiatric intervention. With telemedicine, these patients are now promptly connected to a psychiatrist. Telepsychiatry is primarily focused on emergency departments but it also plays a role in primary care where, fairly regularly, physicians encounter a patient needing a psychiatric evaluation. The typical process has been that the primary care doctor gives the person an appointment to see a psychiatrist but that appointment may well be weeks away. Some patients never make it to the appointment. Now, a physician in the ED can connect the patient to a psychiatrist on the other end of the computer and get immediate help.

"The telehealth opportunity is amazingly disruptive," says Thornton. "It is such a massive opportunity. It's very difficult to wrap your mind around just how big it can be. Patients are going to use it to find doctors. They won't go to the ED any longer. They'll just get a telehealth consult. It's going to be everywhere."

Dr. Martin Doerfler envisions expanding telemedicine capabilities for a variety of situations where it would be more efficient for patient and doctor to connect via computer. The goal, he says, is to be able to use "telehealth for any patient anywhere for any need including educating patients about various conditions including diabetes and heart disease or helping a young mother trying to understand whether she is nursing her baby correctly. Rather than have her get in a car and drive to someone's office you could connect on her iPad and show her the best way to do it in the privacy of her bedroom." An article in Health Affairs noted that telehealth can also "bring medical care into communities with limited access to providers or facilities, reduce wait times, and improve convenience," but that to do so it "requires integration into a *well-functioning* health care system that has the capacity to address all the additional patient needs that telehealth generates"[4].

"There is a care-delivery side to Northwell, and then there is a business-solutions side to Northwell."

Of the 62,000 employees at Northwell, a grand total of 15 of them work within a unit called Northwell Ventures. The team, which is led by Thornton, identifies areas of particular expertise within Northwell and sells those products or skills as business solutions to other health care provider organizations. The Ventures team also looks for investments throughout the health care universe.

What is a not-for-profit organization with a real mission doing swimming with the venture sharks? With major government and commercial payers steadily and often aggressively reducing reimbursements there is the need to find new sources of revenue to compensate for some of the cuts. Revenue from the Ventures business is an important replacement for reduced reimbursements from other sources, mostly government payers. Northwell Ventures is in the business of both making money to compensate for reduced government payments while at the same time advancing ambulatory initiatives. "Reimbursements for clinical care are under tremendous pressure and will continue to be pushed down," says Mark Solazzo. "Government is the majority payer and they are leading the way on how commercial payers act. Medicare payments are down each year while costs rise. Union contracts, supplies, pharmaceuticals are all going up so there is a negative trend gap." Solazzo says the Northwell system can reduce costs through efficiencies by 1 or 2 percent annually and that growth accounts for an additional 2 percent, but to stay positive—Northwell currently makes a margin of about 1.5 percent a year—he has to find additional sources of revenue and a contribution from the venture business could be significant.

Northwell Ventures came about when a major consultancy conducting an analysis within Northwell declared that some of the system's internal operations were among the best in class—for example, physician billing, supply chain, call center management, etc. It became clear that there was an opportunity to package these skills in product form and sell them to other provider organizations. It makes perfect sense, says Thornton. "You are acquiring all of these hospitals, consolidating marketing, legal, finance, revenue cycle, and patient access and in so doing you are reducing overall expense and standardizing them throughout the system," he says. "The point here is that there is a care-delivery side to Northwell and then there is a business-solutions side to Northwell. In the mission of providing care we have developed capabilities others wanted to buy. The epiphany is that the system is where all the ideas" for venture possibilities come from. "We are focused on the development of ambulatory infrastructure. This is everything from urgent care to ambulatory-surgery centers, dialysis centers, lightweight and freestanding emergency departments—low-cost venues of care convenient to our consumers."

Thornton came to Northwell after a number of years leading an innovations group at the Cleveland Clinic. He has worked to build a venture business with multiple aspects to it. One is perhaps the most traditional type of business set up by major hospital groups wherein an employee comes up with an idea, treatment or technology that can be sold to other provider organizations. Many if not most large health care groups stop here and do not attempt to invest in innovation beyond this point, but Thornton says that Northwell pursues a number of other investment approaches including "direct-equity investing in companies either that we have formed or that are external to our organization with the intent of commercializing a capability that we've developed or with the intention of acquiring or sourcing a capability we know we will need to enable our growth strategy." All of these ideas come through the normal course of business within the organization, says Thornton. Typically, he says, doctors at Northwell come to him reporting on small companies, often startups that do something particularly well. The idea of beta testing their product or service in a large system like Northwell is very attractive to these startups. "We take a look at it. Usually they're relatively early stage. We were either a beta or a pilot. The company is desperate for growth capital, desperate for additional customers, desperate for a Northwell case study or story." One such company provides a service doing bundled payment processes for orthopedic services. "The idea was 'why don't we take a look at them as a potential joint-venture investment opportunity,' and this is how we get the vast majority of our deal flow. It's where a technology or a business model *enables our growth strategy*." Thornton and his team are now doing five to seven investments of this kind each year. In the process of developing a business plan, Thornton and his team "came to the conclusion that there is an absolutely massive business opportunity to take our capabilities and to commercialize those in conjunction with a partner." An example involves the complexities of managing all aspects of a physician practice including the payment and billing cycles—collecting payments from many different private insurance companies, from government programs, from individuals—all while insurers do their best to find any excuse to deny payment. "The payments methodologies make revenue cycle extraordinarily expensive," he says, "very, very, very complicated and increasingly health systems outsource this."

As Dowling juggles multiple issues and challenges, he has identified two initiatives in particular which hold the kind of transformative promise that scientists and leaders in health care dream about. One is a joint venture focused on cancer; another, a world-leading initiative in the field of bioelectronic medicine.

Cold Spring Harbor Laboratories

In the course of a career during which he and colleague Francis Crick discovered the DNA double helix, for which they received the Nobel Prize, James Watson held faculty positions at Cambridge, the California Institute of Technology, and Harvard, and his status as one of the iconic scientists of the twentieth century would have assured him a position at any university he chose. But in 1976 he left Harvard and spent the next 40 years at Cold Spring Harbor Laboratory on the north shore of Long Island. On this tranquil water-front campus, breakthrough scientific research has been conducted since 1890. Watson served here as president, chancellor, and, finally, chancellor emeritus, all the while steering "the laboratory into the field of tumor virology, from which emerged our present understanding of [cancer genes] and the molecular basis of cancer"[5].

In the 1990s, Cold Spring Harbor Labs and Northwell Health had little in common. True, they were neighbors on Long Island, but in reality they occupied different spheres in the hierarchy of health care. Under a caste system—and medical science can sometimes resemble one—they would have been in *very* different classes. CSHL was one of the elite institutions in the world led by a man ranked among a handful of the most prominent scientists in history. In contrast, Northwell was a solid, though local, medical group among thousands of such groups in the country. Unsurprisingly, the two organizations had little if anything to do with one another but Michael Dowling wanted to change that. He thought that a collaboration with the Lab would help raise Northwell's capability and status in multiple ways. But why would Cold Spring Harbor Labs want to team up with Northwell? And the answer through the late 1990s and for some years thereafter was, *they wouldn't*. "Cold Spring Harbor Labs was renowned internationally and they were not that interested in joining with us," says Dr. Thomas McGinn, a cancer specialist at Northwell. "Ten years ago or more there was nothing at Northwell for them to engage with, but in the last five to seven years, with the opening of the medical school and the growth of cancer-focused clinician scientists and a comprehensive cancer program, suddenly there was this receiving arm for this lab to talk to."

Over a number of years, Dowling made a point to develop a relationship with Dr. Bruce Stillman, president and CEO of Cold Spring Harbor. Stillman is a renowned scientist in his own right whose research focuses on "the process by which DNA is copied within cells." Dowling got to know Stillman and "worked at nurturing the relationship," says McGinn. "Michael was wooing them for years." Roy Zuckerberg, the former Northwell board chair who remained a trustee, helped bring the two parties together as he had done with the original merger between North Shore University Hospital and Long Island Jewish. Zuckerberg not only served as a trustee at Northwell, he also held a board position at CSHL and thus was familiar with the lead players on both sides.

In 2014, the discussion between Dowling and Stillman became serious in large measure because over time, the two organizations had evolved. Northwell had grown into the

largest health care provider in New York state and one of the
largest in the United States while building a formidable program conducting clinical cancer research and treating patients
with cancer. This involved attracting well-known oncologists
and renovating a massive structure on Long Island to house
every aspect of cancer care. By 2015 Northwell was treating a
comparable number of patients as Memorial Sloan Kettering
and more than New York Presbyterian or Weill Cornell.
"People are always shocked to hear that," says McGinn, "but
the fact was that we became the largest provider of cancer
care services" in the New York-Connecticut-New Jersey region
with approximately 20,000 new cancer cases a year.

The more Dowling and Stillman talked, the more sensible
some sort of affiliation seemed. The two organizations did
not compete on any level so there was no conflict there. Most
importantly, each had what the other needed. Cold Spring
Harbor Laboratory had world-class basic translational cancer
research but no patients. Northwell had tens of thousands of
cancer patients and clinical research. "Here we are next door
to each other, we don't compete on basic scientific stuff, we
have the clinical facility to help translate some of their science
into a health system and we have patients," says McGinn.
"These relationships can work if they are complementing
not competing. We could marry their basic science with our
clinical science, marry these two worlds." As Dr. Lawrence
Smith, Northwell Physician-in-chief put it: "We don't do what
they do and they don't do what we do." Put another way,
Cold Spring Harbor had the bench; Northwell had the bedside. What if you put the two together? After a good deal of
discussion about how this might work, the two organizations
signed a formal agreement in April of 2015. Thus, began their
collaborative effort to get findings from the bench to patients
at the bedside, says Dr. George Raptis, Acting Executive
Director of the Cancer Institute and senior vice president of
the Northwell Cancer Service Line. "They develop things at
a very basic level of science and have an incredible faculty

and they do everything up to just short of getting their findings into the clinic. Where will it lead? Hopefully, faculty in common between the two organizations, more collaborative research, grants, publications, and cures. Our goal is to dramatically change how we treat cancer; to not only to find more cures but to decrease the cost, the financial toxicity of cancer. Better science and more precise cancer diagnostics and therapeutics can potentially drive down the cost. We cannot as a society sustain the current cost of care for patients with cancer and should not accept the modest improvements to date."

A new drug created at Cold Spring Harbor is already being used to treat Northwell patients with breast cancer. Researchers originally thought the drug would be used to treat diabetes but its efficacy there was less than hoped. In early pre-clinical studies in breast cancer patients, however, there are some promising indications. "It alters a novel pathway that blocks cancer cell growth," says McGinn. "It's exciting because it is a totally novel drug based on research done over years at Cold Spring Harbor." Often with such drugs, it is necessary to test them in a number of different clinical locations in order to reach the number of patients required, but because Northwell has so many patients, all of the testing can be done within the system. "We can do it under one roof, coordinate everything," says McGinn, "because of our size and it's really demonstrative of what this relationship can bring. We can integrate across a lot of different areas, collect data efficiently and that is very attractive to these scientists who want to test things in big populations." As this and other trials commence, physicians from Northwell meet regularly with researchers at Cold Spring Harbor to focus on particular types of cancer. Doctors present the researchers with clinical questions about how to attack breast cancer while basic translational researchers then explain what they are doing in the lab that might be useful.

"A lot of it is getting our clinician scientists into the room with their scientists and hope some magic starts to occur," says McGinn. "We come up with patient scenarios, the clinical applicability of their ideas. We've learned how to work together, submitting grants together, testing some of their novel therapies."

"It is very early, but the success is very tangible," says Dr. Kevin Tracey, president of the Feinstein Institute for Medical Research at Northwell. "We have researchers at Cold Spring Harbor meeting regularly with cancer doctors here at Northwell, talking about taking inventions from the lab and putting them into patients and the Cold Spring faculty is collaborating extensively with our Feinstein researchers. In six months we have already launched one of our first joint clinical trials. Merging an integrated system with 20,000 cancer patients annually with historic and powerful research operations is game-changing. Pharmaceutical companies already understand that we have the patient base and the clinical research infrastructure to do big complicated clinical trials. When combined with laboratory authority and experience, it opens all kinds of new doors."

Bioelectronic Medicine

The second initiative that holds such great promise involves what is called bioelectronic medicine and the world leader on this topic happens to be a physician at Northwell. Dr. Kevin Tracey, a neurosurgeon, heads the Feinstein Institute for Medical Research. Through a bit of happenstance in his research one day in the mid-1990s, Tracey stumbled on a discovery that could change the lives of millions of patients. He discovered that a brief electrical impulse applied to a particular nerve could shrink swelling and reduce inflammation. The approach was tested on a group of patients with rheumatoid arthritis, a disabling disease that all but cripples those afflicted. Swollen and painful joints make almost any physical activity difficult or impossible. Typically, such patients are treated with aggressive drugs that, while the drugs work in some cases, they also carry punishing side effects. Tracey's discovery that brief electronic pulses administered to the vagus nerve near the patient's neck block the molecules causing swelling and inflammation have provided hope to these patients. Dr. Tracey wrote about some of the patients in the first round of testing:

> Consider the case of a burly, 47-year-old truck driver from Mostar, Bosnia, Mr. Ostovich has suffered from long-standing rheumatoid arthritis and needed near-permanent bed rest. With his hands and wrists swollen and aching, he could no longer hold on to a wheel or even play with his small children. He tried a variety of medications. None worked. When I met him at his doctor's office in 2012, however, he didn't seem at all afflicted with the disease. That's because, one year earlier, he had been offered the opportunity to be the first participant in a clinical trial of a new therapy based on my invention. He received a bio-electronic implant and rapidly improved. His mobility restored, he was soon back at work and even … playing tennis.

Then there was the case of Mirela, age 38, who was written about in *The New York Times*. She had been diagnosed with rheumatoid arthritis at age 22 and had "tried nine different medications, including two she had to self-inject. Some of them helped but had nasty side effects." The *Times* story noted that before being treated with the electrical pulse conceived by Tracey, "she could barely grasp a pencil; now she's riding her bicycle to the Dutch coast, a near-20-mile round trip from her home." She told *The Times*: "After the implant, I started to do things I hadn't done in years—like taking long walks or just putting clothes on in the morning without help. I was ecstatic … I got my life back."

Delivering the electrical impulses is a relatively simple matter. *The Times* described the process this way[6]:

> The subjects in the trial each underwent a 45-minute operation. A neurosurgeon fixed an inch long device shaped like a corkscrew to the vagus nerve on the left side of the neck, and then embedded just below the collarbone a silver-dollar-size "pulse generator" that contained a battery and microprocessor programmed to discharge mild shocks from two electrodes. A thin wire made of a platinum alloy connected the two components beneath the skin. Once the implant was turned on, its preprogrammed charge—about one milliamp; a small LED consumes 10 times more electricity—zapped the vagus nerve in 60-second bursts, up to four times a day. Typically, a patient's throat felt constricted and tingly for a moment. After a week or two, arthritic pain began to subside. Swollen joints shrank, and blood tests that checked for inflammatory markers usually showed striking declines.

Since 1998, Tracey and his colleagues have published a series of papers in various journals, including *Science* and *Nature*, which demonstrate, as Tracey puts it, "the validity of using electrons to replace drugs." A paper Tracey published in Nature in 2000 reporting his research into bioelectronic medicine has been cited thousands of times and his work has been written about in *The Times*, *Wall Street Journal* and other publications. He was invited to write the cover article in Scientific American. The potential is such that private investors as well as major pharmaceutical companies have invested hundreds of millions of dollars to further develop bioelectronic medicine. No wonder. Tracey believes that it has promise far beyond rheumatoid arthritis. "There is very interesting data that diabetes can be modulated or potentially treated through nerve signals. So that is a major target. Cancer is another. Although this is several years from clinical development, the opportunity to do the research is now. For example, there is already evidence in cancer that neurotransmitters and nerve signaling can control tumor cell growth and metastasis. Moreover, autoimmune disease, rheumatoid arthritis, inflammatory bowel disease, Crohn's disease, and psoriasis are on the list of potential targets because the immunology mechanisms of these syndromes is where we started, and we know what to do. Hypertension is a major target. There are 1 billion hypertensive patients on the planet, and despite the available medications, millions of patients are inadequately treated. Compliance is terrible." He notes that drugs, which in some cases cost tens of thousands of dollars per year, are not effective in all patients and may carry "black-box warnings, which means that death is a possible side effect. Why would a patient pursue a drug regimen when they could opt for a few electronic pulses?" Is it possible that treatments like this, pulses through electronic devices, could replace some drugs in the coming years as preferred treatments? Tracey believes it is and that is perhaps why the pharmaceutical industry closely follows his work. "The potential of this is so staggering," says Dr. Lawrence Smith. "I don't think anyone knows yet how far this can go."

"You have to meld the two concepts of tough business with the community aspect ... "

The wonderful thing about the ubiquity of Einstein's definition of insanity—*doing the same thing over and over again and expecting a different result*—is that it leads to the inescapable conclusion that active learning and change are essential elements of improvement. If you are part of the problem in health care—and who isn't?—that means you have to learn, change, do things differently. In the process of learning comes perspective. In Dowling's case his perspective is a mix of education, personal and professional experience, and constant learning. A crucial element of perspective comes only through adversity. Unless you have faced tough situations, how can you expect to take on the big challenges? Dowling tells a funny story from his days in government when he stood before a hostile crowd in Manhattan boiling about some recent state policy. It was Dowling's job to explain the policy while also taking questions. "In government you have to have perspective and not get thrown off by little things because you get pilloried all the time," he says. "You get criticized all the time. I was walking out of this meeting one night in Manhattan—this was years ago—and people were so angry, shouting at me and all of that. Walking out of the meeting a reporter from *The Times* asked me, 'how do you feel after a meeting like that?' And I said, 'you know, there are days when I feel like the state's fire hydrant.' And he looks at me and says, 'fire hydrant?' And I said, 'yeah, everybody is pissing on me all the time!' It was in *The Times* the next day and the governor said to me, 'fire hydrant, huh?' You roll with the punches. Every fight is 15 rounds and you may lose a couple of rounds but don't worry about it. Just make sure you know where you are going."

As much as possible in this environment, Dowling does know where he is going and he brings his unusual if not unique perspective to bear every Monday morning when, with rare exceptions, he personally addresses the newly hired Northwell employees. Some weeks there are 100, other weeks 200-plus. He welcomes these new hires, bright, eager, ready-to-go, many at or near the start of their careers. He explains to them what the organization is all about, touches upon a variety of issues. He needs these people to be at their best every day if the mission is to be within reach. The organization grows rapidly and as it does Dowling works to try and figure out where all this is headed. The map of the future presents a puzzling array of choices. Do you turn this way or that? How do you balance the mission with the need to stay afloat financially? How do you take care of patients like Vincent when the government pays $150 for the compassion, time and professional expertise of a half dozen physicians, PhDs, and nurses?

He does not say this during the Monday morning orientation but Dowling knows that to be part of the solution he has to strengthen his organization so that it has muscle and scale. He has assembled a complete delivery system with primary care through the end of life, home care, 400 ambulatory care centers and counting, hospice—"the whole continuum all integrated." But the financial pressure is brutal. His margin is 1.5 percent per year or so and every once in a while he will remind his board members that he could increase that up to "5 or 6 percent but I would have to close my psychiatric hospitals which are losing $40 million a year, and close the innovation center. I would get rid of research—a $100 million loss a year. But now you are not pursuing discovery for new medical treatments. I could get rid of psychiatric facilities but then what about the people who are in dire need? We have to make a margin that allows me to do things that do not make money—that lose money, in fact—so that I can sleep at night knowing that I am providing comprehensive care people need. It is different from what a regular business would do. I don't care about that. I have multiple metrics. Open access, taking care of everybody, respecting everybody. We run a number of programs for veterans and we pay for them because I believe dealing with veterans is important. That is what community is about. That is why you have to meld the two concepts of tough business with the community aspect of what we are all about. If you travel around the country you find that there are hospitals where there are no emergency rooms—even in New York that is true at some places. I don't think that is right. I just don't think that's right. I'd rather make a 1 percent margin, a 2 percent margin and do the right things than make a 6 percent margin and not do the right things. That is the balance and a lot of the big systems in the country don't do a lot of the things we do."

"Opening the aperture."

In June of 2016 at the Montauk gathering, the focus was
on the real mission and how that mission relates to the
hospitals suffering from financial and other ills in central
Brooklyn. Prior to the Montauk meeting, Northwell leaders
were already working on the matter and, within four months,
Jeff Kraut, with the help of 60 additional people, had completed a 145-page plan for how to address the Brooklyn challenges. This was, by any definition, an immense problem
that had only grown more acute in recent years. These five
hospitals[7]—individually and collectively—were hemorrhag-
ing money. A year earlier, five of these institutions[8] collectively lost nearly $500 million. They had been unable to afford
any meaningful capital improvements for a decade or more
and the overwhelming majority of their revenue came from
patients on Medicaid. One of the hospitals had twice declared
bankruptcy while prior attempts at a merger of three of the
hospitals failed. These hospitals were serving communities
with some of the worst health outcomes and socioeconomic
determinants of health anywhere and in the face of those
challenges the community was experiencing a shortage of
doctors, pharmacies and places to purchase fresh food. "It's
an economically depressed area," says Kraut. "It has a hyper
concentration, in parts of it, of public housing associated with
people of poverty and low literacy rates and high crime rates."

Officials at the state health department and within the
governor's office had, for some time, been searching for a
solution. Having watched Northwell absorb a number of new
hospitals of varying types and sizes into its network, the
government officials believed that the Northwell experience
was applicable to the Brooklyn situation. The assignment to
Northwell, says Kraut, boiled down to "the state saying to us,
'tell us what Northwell would do with these Brooklyn organizations as you have done with others. No one else in the
state has done what you've done. You've taken hospitals that
were losing money and turned them around and developed

relationships with both the communities and the unions in doing these things.' That is not to say we haven't had bumps in the road. We definitely have but the fact is that we do have experience and understanding of what it takes to bring hospitals together, to get them to work together."

And here is a crucial piece: Kraut, Dowling and their many Northwell colleagues had experience getting individual hospitals to think in terms not only of their own interests, but of the broader interests of the system and that was key to moving forward in Brooklyn. Kraut referred to it as "opening the aperture" so that "instead of looking at their own little piece, to look beyond it and to look into the greater good of the community, to widen the aperture to see what their broader responsibilities are." State government was making a commitment to support the operations of these hospitals to the extent of $1.5 billion over five years, and provide an additional $700 million to create and transform a regional health care delivery system. Between the time of the Montauk meeting in June and the writing of his report in October, Kraut and his team met with residents, local elected officials from the city council, assembly and senate, staff members from the hospitals, community leaders, clergy, union leaders, officials from the city and state departments of health, and staff from the governor's office. The difficult but realistic conclusion that Kraut and his colleagues reached was that "the market and financial forces confronting these hospitals make it virtually impossible for them to succeed as stand-alone hospitals." Kraut and his colleagues studied each hospital individually while examining the overall needs of the neighborhood and they settled on a standard for any recommendations they were considering proposing. The test involved opening the aperture: Was it in the best interest of the community overall; not was it in the best interest of one particular hospital, or one neighborhood, or one political constituency. Was it good for the *whole community*. "There has to be a regional view," says Kraut. "You cannot just look at this and ask, 'is this going to

hurt my hospital. Is it going to hurt another hospital?' They
have overlapping service areas. These hospitals are within a
few minutes of each other. The community just doesn't need
that many hospitals. You have to look in the region and ask
what does the region need the most?" The answer to that
question was neighborhood access to more primary care
doctors.

"The plan would consolidate these institutions into one
entity, reduce redundancies, rebuild one hospital and expand
the ambulatory network," says Mark Solazzo. "The political components of the plan are really hard but this is a great
opportunity to decrease costs, become more efficient, and
reduce the government subsidy."

The report proposed radically reshaping the way care was
delivered while at the same time making new recommendations that spoke to the broader social and economic needs of
the area. "The people in the community love their hospitals
but they were spot on about what they needed and that is
ambulatory care," says Kraut. "The transformative investment
is not fixing the hospital, it is building an ambulatory care
network." At the end of his study and analysis, Kraut wrote a
145-page report with a series of recommendations. The proposal called for dividing up responsibility among the hospitals
for different clinical areas. For example, one of the hospitals
(Brookdale) "would get built up as kind of the acute tertiary
hospital." Another (Interfaith) would focus on both community access to medical and surgical care and behavioral
health needs. The idea was to provide all the services needed
by the residents of the area, but not to duplicate services at
various locations. The proposal also called for installing the
latest technology "so that as a patient no matter where you
are touched in this community—no matter what hospital or
ambulatory care center—all your health data is moving with
you." The plan also called for a significant infusion of funding
for capital improvements in all the facilities. Kraut was acutely
sensitive throughout the process to the fact that these hospitals

employ about 8000 people in the Brooklyn neighborhoods. These jobs are essential to the community's sustainability. The addition of a more robust ambulatory network would create about 880 new jobs in clinics while improving access to care and increasing the number of doctors in the area. Kraut's blueprint essentially guaranteed that "everybody has a job today will have a job" under the new plan "just not maybe the same job." Would this be disruptive for some people? Yes. Was it in the best interest of the community overall? Definitely.

Perhaps the most exciting aspect of the proposal was its call for hiring 120 new primary and specialty care physicians to help create a network with office locations scattered throughout the area. The front lines of the network would be small practices of three or four physicians anchored by an urgent care center that takes care of their patients after hours so they don't go to an ED and that pod is connected to specialty care for radiology, ambulatory surgery, and specialized procedures. Recruiting 120 new doctors was no easy matter. "How do you do that?" Kraut asked. "How do you get them there? How do you build facilities for them?" Part of the answer is thinking more broadly about various elements, including social determinants of health, that the government can help shape. For example, is it possible to use tax policy or housing policy or loan forgiveness to draw new physicians into the neighborhoods? Kraut, Dowling and their colleagues at Northwell believe it is. Mark Solazzo says that for long-term success the entire central Brooklyn area should be designated as a "health care enterprise zone" where federal funds help with development that enables construction of housing, some with an urgent care center occupying the first floor, and creating jobs for residents. Kraut and his team met with the commissioner of housing for New York state and proposed that "for every housing project that's going up, whoever the developers have chosen, they should be incented by either zoning bonuses, density or economic bonuses to work, that if they do work with us and we plan and build our ambulatory care units into those new buildings, so they're integrated with the housing."

Kraut and the Northwell team were, at heart, proposing the creation of an "economic development, a health enterprise zone" which would use tax and housing policy to encourage creation and expansion of job-creating businesses and affordable housing. For physicians who relocate in the community it was proposed that there would be an exemption from state and city taxes along with loan forgiveness and affordable housing. "We wanted to hardwire into that in making decisions for this area the government would always consider new funding and programs in the context of health care policy in every action they take. It goes back to the social obligation, the moral obligation of the system. It's Michael the social worker."

The reaction to the proposal has generally been positive, although there has been some strong pushback against various elements of the plan. The idea of a unified board has not gone over particularly well. "That was the most controversial recommendation," says Kraut. "We knew that everybody would hate it but it is key" to a more regional view; opening the aperture to see what is good for all, not one particular organization.[9]

During a meeting of the Northwell Health Board of Trustees in late January 2017, Michael Dowling was asked by board chair Mark Claster why the organization had conducted the Brooklyn study—"what was our purpose?" Claster asked. Dowling replied:

> Well, from a business point of view, it's minimal at the moment. I'm a strong believer that with a large system with such a big footprint as ours we should not shy away from helping or to figure out what to do in very underserved communities. If we are afraid to deal and delve into some of these things, if we are afraid to provide assistance, not to take responsibility but to be of assistance, I don't think this is what

Northwell stands for. Sharing our experience, expertise and insights—where we can provide benefit and
strengthen the health care delivery system in New
York—this is what Northwell stands for and should be.

We have to be community focused or we are not
real. And the other thing is, a lot of the people, all
of the people that Jeff [Kraut] mentioned who con-
tributed to the study, by being in that community
and working on this project allowed staff to learn an
awful lot about the other side of the world. That, in
and of itself, is an amazing and valuable education.
Now we have pockets of worlds like this scattered
around our system but we have yet to confront the
issues we have encountered in central Brooklyn.
When you are in parts of Brooklyn, sometimes you
think you are in a third world environment when it
comes to providing healthcare.

And to the extent that Northwell can be a good
citizen of the City of New York, and helping as much
as we can with our talent to improve the well-being
of all New Yorkers, I think it is a pot of our gold—it
is important and it is part of our mission. We worry
about communities in Africa and in India and other
places … these … are 20 to 30 minutes away … and
I think for the staff in our organization, including
many of our staff that have been very gifted with
privilege and not exposed to the challenges these
communities have to confront, to … focus on something like that is a worthwhile project; that is the
return of the investment of our time and resources
and Northwell will be benefitted as an organization
in the long term.

Someone in government asked Dowling how long it would
take to accomplish the changes in Brooklyn and he replied that
it would require seven years. "They said, 'why can't you do it

next year?' I said, 'it doesn't work like that. You are changing 50 years of culture, ingrained strategies that are built into every nook and cranny of that place and those particular hospitals.'" It was not the answer they wanted to hear, but it was the truth, and the hard truth is that if you are going to be part of the solution in health care you must take on the challenges like the one in Brooklyn. You must do all of the other things well, of course—have great quality and access in your hospitals and clinics, but you must also place greater emphasis on public health.

Age of Discovery

Two or three times each year, Dowling sends out a brief memo to his leadership team with reading recommendations. You would expect that the books he recommends would be generally focused on health care, broadly or specifically, but that is not Dowling. In late 2016 here was his list with the note he attached to each one:

> **City of Dreams**: *The 400-year epic history of immigrant New York* By Tyler Anbinder.
> This is one of the best books I have ever read—especially if you have an interest in history. It's 600 pages but worth it. Whatever your background, this will inform you more and also put some of the current immigration debate in historical perspective.

> **The Fractured Republic** By Yuval Levin
> A great book to better understand the present environment. It discusses the politics of nostalgia—how we often wish for a past which can blind us to what we need to do now. Very worthwhile reading.

> **Age of Discovery** By Ian Goldin and Chris Kutarna
> A stimulating read that uses the innovations of the Renaissance period to put our current developments

in perspective. You will enjoy and be much more educated.

Competing Against Luck By Clayton Christensen You are familiar with his other books such as the Innovators Dilemma. This book discusses customer service and innovation from another perspective. It's different and provocative.

These selections are intriguing. The book about New York makes perfect sense for it is, after all, home turf for Northwell and it is a place with a rich history of immigrant accomplishment, Dowling included. *The Fractured Republic* speaks to the turbulent political times while the Clayton Christensen book is another in the series by one of the more accomplished business thinkers of our age. Perhaps the most revealing of these titles recommended by Dowling is *The Age of Discovery* for this is a book that transcends regions, commerce, or politics. It celebrates the great period of enlightenment—the breakthroughs from da Vinci, Michelangelo, Copernicus, and Gutenberg. This recommendation carries a clear message: Yes, times are tough and complicated but great things lie ahead—as the book suggests: "*This is the best moment in history to be alive.*" Dowling's recommendation suggests not only his long-held desire to learn, but also helps define his optimism about the future. He knows that the challenges from patients like Vincent and the millions of Vincents out there will not be dealt with easily just as he knows how difficult it will be to bring equity, access, quality, and affordability to those Brooklyn neighborhoods and other communities like them. But he celebrates the effort and the journey and the mission that he and his team are on. And he believes, as he strains to peer over the horizon, that he and his colleagues will get that much closer to achieving the real mission.

Endnotes

1. The Commonwealth Fund; "How high-need patients experience the health care system in nine countries," by Dana O.
   Sarnak and Jamie Ryan, January 11, 2016.
2. "How does growth in health care costs affect the American
   family?" by David I. Auerbach, Arthur L. Kellermann; RAND
   Corporation; http://www.rand.org/pubs/research_briefs/
   RB9605.html.
3. Health Affairs Blog, "New health care symposium: Reimagining
   the health care industry," by Michael Dowling, March 4, 2016.
4. Health Affairs Blog, "Telehealth alone will not increase health
   care access for the underserved," by Lori Uscher-Pines and
   Ateev Mehrotra, December 15, 2016; http://healthaffairs.org/
   blog/2016/12/15/telehealth-alone-will-not-increase-health-care-
   access-for-the-underserved/.
5. Cold Spring Harbor Laboratory; http://www.cshl.edu/.
6. *The New York Times Magazine*, "Can the nervous system be
   hacked?" by Michael Behar, May 23, 2014; https://www.nytimes.
   com/2014/05/25/magazine/can-the-nervous-system-be-hacked.
   html.
7. Brookdale University Hospital and Medical Center, Kingsbrook
   Jewish Medical Center, Interfaith Medical Center, Wyckoff
   Heights Medical Center, and University Hospital Brooklyn.
8. Wyckoff, Interfaith, Kingsbrook, Brookdale, and Downstate in
   Flatbush.
9. "The Brooklyn Study: Reshaping the Future of Healthcare:
   Restructuring and investing in healthcare delivery in the communities of central and northeastern Brooklyn." A Report to the
   Department of Health of New York state. Transmitted October
   2016. Northwell Health contracted to conduct the study for payment of $400,000 aware that the total cost to Northwell of the
   work would be well in excess of $1 million.

Index

400-year epic history of immigrant New York, 216
9/11, 106, 107

A

Abrams, Kenneth, 145, 146
Adelphi University, 34
Affordable Care Act, 178
Agency for Healthcare Research and Quality (AHRQ), 40, 41
Age of Discovery, 216–217
AHRQ, *see* Agency for Healthcare Research and Quality (AHRQ)
al-Qaeda, 98
American Airlines flight 587, 107
American College of Health Care, 53
American medical schools, 61, 62
Anbinder, Tyler, 216
Aristotle, 10

B

Barger, Michael, 37–38, 39, 40
Battinelli, David, 63, 66–69, 71–79, 82–84, 86, 89, 91, 134
Berlin, Isaiah, viii–ix
Berwick, Donald, 155

bin Laden, Osama, 99
Bioelectronic medicine, 204–216
Bioskills Center, 93
Bisognano, Maureen, 155
Blue Cross, 9, 27
Blumenthal, David, 136
Boal, Jeremy, 163
Boston City Hospital, 63
Boston University Medical Center, 63
Boston University School of Medicine, 63
A Bridge to Quality, 41
British Medical Journal, 74
Brooklyn, 1, 2, 210, 213, 214–216

C

Cancer care, 202–203
CareConnect, 177–187
Care value, 171–187
Carlyle, Thomas, 34
Carnegie Foundation, 93
Carnegie Foundation for the Advancement of Teaching, 60, 61, 66
Casalino, Lawrence P., 136
Case-based curriculum, 86–93
Catholic Medical Center, 99
CDC, *see* Centers for Disease Control (CDC)

Center for Learning and
    Education, 93
Center for Learning and Innovation
    (CLI), 42–43, 47, 49–53,
    55–56, 65, 83, 92, 103,
    112, 160
Centers for Disease Control (CDC),
    113, 114, 166, 167
Christensen, Clayton, 217
Claster, Mark, 214
Cleveland Clinic, 198
CLI, *see* Center for Learning and
    Innovation (CLI)
Clinton, Bill, 9
CNN, 49
Code Sepsis, 150, 159
Cold Spring Harbor Laboratories
    (CSHL), 200–204
Commonwealth Fund, 117, 136
Community Paramedic Program,
    182–183
Competing Against Luck, 217
Conigliaro, Joseph, 122–128, 131,
    137, 139
Consumer Price Index, 193
Cooke, Molly, 69
Crew Resource Management, 38,
    39, 40, 51
Crick, Francis, 200
Crossing the Quality Chasm, 155
Crosson, Francis J., 136
Crotonville educational approach, 32
CSHL, *see* Cold Spring Harbor
    Laboratories (CSHL)
Culture clash, 20–23
Cuomo, Andrew, 164, 165
Cuomo, Mario M., 4, 7–11, 13, 32
Czura, Christopher J., 143

D

D'Angelo, John, 144, 147, 148, 150,
    158, 159, 161, 165

Davis, Lawrence, 45
Department of Defense, 40
Department of Radiology, 45
Dlugacz, Yosef, 129
Doerfler, Martin, 142–143,
    145–148, 151–153, 155–157,
    159–164, 197
Dowling, Dennis, 21, 25
Dowling, Michael, x, 1–3, 4–13,
    17–19, 22, 24, 26–32, 33,
    35, 37, 49, 53–56, 59–65,
    96–98, 102, 105, 108–109,
    113, 142–144, 154, 162, 165,
    172, 174, 176–178, 185–186,
    189–195, 200–202,
    207–209, 214, 216, 217
Driver diagram, 156

E

Ebola, 111, 112, 113
Edelstein, Martin, 21
Eisenhower, Dwight David, 38
Electronic Medical Records
    (EMR), 136
Elkowitz, David, 86, 88
Emergency Departments and
    Critical Care, 163
Emergency management, 102–103
Emergency Medical Technician
    (EMT), 73
Empire Blue Cross, 12
EMR, *see* Electronic Medical
    Records (EMR)
EMT, *see* Emergency Medical
    Technician (EMT)

F

F/A-18 Hornet fighter jet, 38
Farmer, Paul, 2
*Fatal Sequence: The Killer
    Within*, 143

Feinstein Institute of Medical
    Research, 143
*The Fifth Discipline: The Art and
    Practice of the Learning
    Organization*, 36
Flexner, Abraham, 59–65, 68–69,
    76, 77, 93
Fordham University, 30
Ford Motor Company, 36
Formative assessment, 83
The Fractured Republic, 216, 217

G

Gallagher, Jack, 16, 17, 18, 19, 24,
    26, 27
Gallo, Kathy, 33–45, 52–56, 92,
    95–100, 107–108, 112, 160
GE, 32
Giuliani, Rudolph, 97
Glen Cove Hospital, 25, 112,
    113, 159
Global Sepsis Alliance, 143
Gold, Howard, 9–11, 13, 18, 19,
    26–27, 173, 174–175, 184,
    187, 194–195
Goldin, Ian, 216
Goldman Sachs, 17
Graduate Nursing and Physician
    Assistant Studies, 92
Gross Domestic Product, 193

H

Hartford Hospital, 41
Harvard School of Public Health, 35
Harvard T.H. Chan School of Public
    Health, 33
Health Affairs, 197
Health care, 31, 41, 49, 55
Health care enterprise zone,
    213, 214
Health insurance, 8–9

Health Solutions, 179
"The Hedgehog and the Fox", viii
Helmreich, Robert L., 40, 41
Hippocrates, 142
Hirsh, Bruce, 153
Hofstra Northwell School of
    Medicine, 46, 59–93
Hofstra School of Law, 64
Hospital for Special Surgery, 33
House Calls program, 181, 183
Humphrey, Hubert, 9

I

ICE, *see* Initial clinical experience
    (ICE)
IHI, *see* Institute for Healthcare
    Improvement (IHI)
Immelt, Jeff, 32–33
Independent at Home program, 181
Initial clinical experience (ICE), 77
Institute for Healthcare
    Improvement (IHI),
    154–155, 156, 157, 158, 159
Institute of Medicine, 40, 115, 155
Insurance companies, 9, 172–174,
    176–179, 184, 185, 186
Irby, David M., 69

J

Jamaica Plain Veterans
    Administration Medical
    Center, 63
Jarrett, Mark, 118, 132–133, 135, 137
JetBlue University, 37
John F. Kennedy International
    Airport, 29, 107
John M. Eisenberg Award, 163
Joint Commission, 163
*Joint Commission Journal on
    Quality and Patient
    Safety*, 163

K

Kabcenell, Andrea, 157
Kaiser Permanente, 92–93, 178
Kanzer, Barry, 45–48, 51
Katz, Saul, 16–18
Kaufman, Robert, 18
Kerner, Robert, 43
KLM 747, 38
Kowalczyk, Walter, 100
Krasnoff, Abraham, 129
Kraut, Jeff, 17, 21, 24, 28, 55, 210–211, 213–215
Kutarna, Chris, 216

L

Learning obsession, 29–57
Lee, Thomas, 180
Lenox Hill Hospital, 135
Levin, Yuval, 216
Life-saving steps, 150–160
LIJ, *see* Long Island Jewish Medical Center (LIJ)
Lombardi, Vince, 161
Long Island Jewish Forest Hills Hospital, 49, 51
Long Island Jewish Medical Center (LIJ), 16–23, 25, 45

M

McGinn, Thomas, 201–204
Master of Science Program, 92
Medical education, 59–60, 65, 76
Medical schools, 68–76
Merinoff Symposium, 143, 163
Mobile Integrated Health, *see* Community Paramedic Program
Mobile Intensive Care Units, 104
Mortality, 161
Mosaic concept, 24–26

Moscola, Joe, 54
Mount Sinai School of Medicine, 63, 119
Murray, Alan, 177–178

N

Nappi, Ralph, 16, 17, 18, 19, 25
Nash, Ira, 128, 129, 130, 136
National Family Council on Sepsis, 167
National Institutes of Health, 145
National Quality Forum, 163
National Transportation Safety Board, 107
Nature, 206
Navy Fighter Weapons School, 38
New England Journal of Medicine, 76, 84, 93, 180
Newman, Josh, 74, 88
New York Air National Guard, 55
New York City Fire Department, 97, 98
New York City Police Department, 101
New York Mets, 16
The New York Times, 6, 9, 21–23, 113, 163, 165, 205–206, 208
New York University Langone Medical Center, 111
North Shore University Hospital, 12, 16, 17–18, 20, 21, 23, 25, 33–34, 53, 129
Northwell ED Sepsis algorithm, 161
Northwell Health, 1, 3, 11, 25–26, 28, 29, 32–35, 39, 52, 54, 56, 62–63, 142–144, 155, 163, 175, 186, 192, 194, 200–202, 215
Northwell Health Board of Trustees, 214

Northwell Health Physician
       Partners, 128
Northwell Ventures, 197–198

O

O'Neill, Brian, 97, 100, 103, 104
O'Neill, John, 95–98, 106, 107

P

Pan American 747, 38
Parmentier, Darlene, 147, 159
Partners in Health, 2
Patient-centered explorations in
       active reasoning, learning,
       and synthesis (PEARLS),
       86–88
Patient Safety and Quality, 163
Patient Safety Institute, 52
PDSA, *see* Plan–Do–Study–Act
       (PDSA) approach
PEARLS, *see* Patient-centered
       explorations in active
       reasoning, learning, and
       synthesis (PEARLS)
Pilapil, Mariecel, 116–121, 127, 128
Plan–Do–Study–Act (PDSA)
       approach, 159
Population health, 66
Porter, Michael, x, 180
Press Ganey Co., 129

Q

Quality, in health care, 115–117,
       123–124, 127, 172

R

Rabinowitz, Stuart, 63–64
Raju, Ram, 190
RAND Corporation analysis, 193

Raptis, George, 202
Romagnoli, Jim, 101, 105, 109
Roosevelt, Theodore, 38
"Rory's Regulations", 165
Rory Staunton Foundation for
       Sepsis Prevention, 164, 167
Rosen, Robert A., 95

S

Safer Healthcare, 39
Sandy (storm), 108
Scanlon, Robert, 79–82
Schulman, Joseph, 179–180,
       182–183
Senge, Peter, 36
Sepsis, 142–144, 146–150, 153, 158,
       160, 163, 166
Sepsis Alliance, 163
Seton Hall–Hackensack School, 93
Shore, David, 32–33, 35
Simone, Amanda, 121, 122
Simulation, 39–56
SIRS, *see* Systemic Inflammatory
       Response Syndrome (SIRS)
Six Sigma, 36–37
Smith, Ben, 79, 80, 81, 82
Smith, Kris, 131, 179–183
Smith, Larry, 64, 65, 86
Smith, Lawrence, x, 2–3, 23, 63,
       66–69, 70–79, 82–84, 86,
       89, 91, 93, 134, 136–138,
       171, 173–175, 202, 207
Smith, Miriam A., 49–52
Society for Simulation in
       Healthcare, 44
Solazzo, Mark, 3, 9, 11, 13, 21–22,
       24, 29, 102, 105, 108–109,
       112, 129, 144, 151, 176, 186,
       194, 198, 212, 213
Southside Hospital, 109
Squires, David, 136
Stanton, Bonnie Bonita, 93

Staten Island University Hospital, 105, 109

Staunton, Orlaith, 166

Staunton, Rory, 141

STEPPS, *see* Strategies and Tools to Enhance Performance and Patient Safety (STEPPS)

Stillman, Bruce, 201, 202

Strategies and Tools to Enhance Performance and Patient Safety (STEPPS), 40–41

Strauss, Scott, 106

Summative assessment, 83

Surviving Sepsis campaign, 146, 155, 161

Systemic Inflammatory Response Syndrome (SIRS), 149, 150

T

Taming Sepsis Educational Program, 160

Tangney, Gene, 40, 97–100, 102, 104, 105, 111–112

Telehealth, 197

Telemedicine, 196, 197

Telepsychiatry, 196

Thornton, Thomas, 196–199

Time zero, concept of, 153

To Err Is Human, 155

TOPGUN, 38

Toyota Production System lean management approach, 37

Tracey, Kevin, 143, 163, 204–207

Traditional medical schools, 65

Triple Aim, 66

Trusting relationship, 124

Tuck School of Business, 70

U

United States Agency for Healthcare Research and Quality, 115

United States Department of Justice, 19–20

University College Cork, 5, 6

University of Miami, 41

University of Pennsylvania, 38

University of Pittsburgh School of Medicine, 41

University of Rochester, 63

V

VISICU, 145

W

Watson, James, 200

"Weapons of Mass Destruction, Implications in Healthcare", 98

Welch, Jack, 36

World Trade Center, 96, 105

World Trade (film), 106

Y

Yousef, Ramzi, 96

Z

Zuckerberg, Roy, 16, 17, 201